FTCE Earth/Space Science 6-12

Teacher Certification Exam

By: Sharon Wynne, M.S.
Southern Connecticut State University

"And, while there's no reason yet to panic, I think it's only prudent that we make preparations to panic."

XAMonline, INC.

Boston

XAMonline, Inc.
25 First St. Suite 106
Cambridge. MA 02141
Toll Free: 1-800-509-4128
Email: info@xamonline.com
Web: www.xamonline.com
Fax: 1-781-662-9268

Library of Congress Cataloging-in-Publication Data

Wynne, Sharon A.
    Earth/Space Science 6-12: Teacher Certification / Sharon A. Wynne. -3rd ed.
    ISBN 978-1-60787-004-3
    1. Earth/Space Science 6-12.   2. Study Guides.   3. FTCE
    4. Teachers' Certification & Licensure.   5. Careers

Disclaimer:
The opinions expressed in this publication are the sole works of XAMonline and were created independently from the National Education Association, Educational Testing Service, or any State Department of Education, National Evaluation Systems or other testing affiliates.

Between the time of publication and printing, state specific standards as well as testing formats and website information may change that is not included in part or in whole within this product. Sample test questions are developed by XAMonline and reflect similar content as on real tests; however, they are not former tests. XAMonline assembles content that aligns with state standards but makes no claims nor guarantees teacher candidates a passing score. Numerical scores are determined by testing companies such as NES or ETS and then are compared with individual state standards. A passing score varies from state to state.

Printed in the United States of America   œ-1

FTCE: Earth/Space Science 6-12
ISBN: 978-1-60787-004-3

Table of Contents

Great Study and Testing Tips!

What to study in order to prepare for the subject assessments is the focus of this study guide but equally important is *how* you study.

You can increase your chances of truly mastering the information by taking some simple, but effective steps.

Study Tips:

1. Some foods aid the learning process. Foods such as milk, nuts, seeds, rice, and oats help your study efforts by releasing natural memory enhancers called CCKs (*cholecystokinin*) composed of *tryptopha*n, *choline*, and *phenylalanine*. All of these chemicals enhance the neurotransmitters associated with memory. Before studying, try a light, protein-rich meal of eggs, turkey, and fish. All of these foods release the memory enhancing chemicals. The better the connections, the more you comprehend.

Likewise, before you take a test, stick to a light snack of energy boosting and relaxing foods. A glass of milk, a piece of fruit, or some peanuts all release various memory-boosting chemicals and help you to relax and focus on the subject at hand.

2. Learn to take great notes. A by-product of our modern culture is that we have grown accustomed to getting our information in short doses (i.e. TV news sound bites or USA Today style newspaper articles.)

Consequently, we've subconsciously trained ourselves to assimilate information better in neat little packages. If your notes are scrawled all over the paper, it fragments the flow of the information. Strive for clarity. Newspapers use a standard format to achieve clarity. Your notes can be much clearer through use of proper formatting. A very effective format is called the *"Cornell Method."*

> Take a sheet of loose-leaf lined notebook paper and draw a line all the way down the paper about 1-2" from the left-hand edge.

> Draw another line across the width of the paper about 1-2" up from the bottom. Repeat this process on the reverse side of the page.

Look at the highly effective result. You have ample room for notes, a left hand margin for special emphasis items or inserting supplementary data from the textbook, a large area at the bottom for a brief summary, and a little rectangular space for just about anything you want.

3. <u>Get the concept then the details</u>. Too often we focus on the details and don't gather an understanding of the concept. However, if you simply memorize only dates, places, or names, you may well miss the whole point of the subject.

A key way to understand things is to put them in your own words. If you are working from a textbook, automatically summarize each paragraph in your mind. If you are outlining text, don't simply copy the author's words.

Rephrase them in your own words. You remember your own thoughts and words much better than someone else's, and subconsciously tend to associate the important details to the core concepts.

4. <u>Ask Why?</u> Pull apart written material paragraph by paragraph and don't forget the captions under the illustrations.

Example: If the heading is "Stream Erosion", flip it around to read "Why do streams erode?" Then answer the questions.

If you train your mind to think in a series of questions and answers, not only will you learn more, but it also helps to lessen the test anxiety because you are used to answering questions.

5. <u>Read for reinforcement and future needs</u>. Even if you only have 10 minutes, put your notes or a book in your hand. Your mind is similar to a computer; you have to input data in order to have it processed. *By reading, you are creating the neural connections for future retrieval.* The more times you read something, the more you reinforce the learning of ideas.

Even if you don't fully understand something on the first pass, *your mind stores much of the material for later recall.*

6. <u>Relax to learn so go into exile</u>. Our bodies respond to an inner clock called biorhythms. Burning the midnight oil works well for some people, but not everyone.

If possible, set aside a particular place to study that is free of distractions. Shut off the television, cell phone, pager and exile your friends and family during your study period.

If you really are bothered by silence, try background music. Light classical music at a low volume has been shown to aid in concentration over other types. Music that evokes pleasant emotions without lyrics are highly suggested. Try just about anything by Mozart. It relaxes you.

7. <u>Use arrows not highlighters</u>. At best, it's difficult to read a page full of yellow, pink, blue, and green streaks. Try staring at a neon sign for a while and you'll soon see that the horde of colors obscure the message.

A quick note, a brief dash of color, an underline, and an arrow pointing to a particular passage is much clearer than a horde of highlighted words.

8. <u>Budget your study time</u>. Although you shouldn't ignore any of the material, *allocate your available study time in the same ratio that topics may appear on the test.*

Testing Tips:

1. <u>Get smart, play dumb</u>. Don't read anything into the question. Don't make an assumption that the test writer is looking for something else than what is asked. Stick to the question as written and don't read extra things into it.

2. <u>Read the question and all the choices *twice* before answering the</u> <u>question</u>. You may miss something by not carefully reading, and then re-reading both the question and the answers.

If you really don't have a clue as to the right answer, leave it blank on the first time through. Go on to the other questions, as they may provide a clue as to how to answer the skipped questions.

If later on, you still can't answer the skipped ones . . . ***Guess.*** The only penalty for guessing is that you *might* get it wrong. Only one thing is certain; if you don't put anything down, you will get it wrong!

3. <u>Turn the question into a statement</u>. Look at the way the questions are worded. The syntax of the question usually provides a clue. Does it seem more familiar as a statement rather than as a question? Does it sound strange?

By turning a question into a statement, you may be able to spot if an answer sounds right, and it may also trigger memories of material you have read.

4. <u>Look for hidden clues</u>. It's actually very difficult to compose multiple-foil (choice) questions without giving away part of the answer in the options presented.

In most multiple-choice questions you can often readily eliminate one or two of the potential answers. This leaves you with only two real possibilities and automatically your odds go to Fifty-Fifty for very little work.

5. <u>Trust your instincts</u>. For every fact that you have read, you subconsciously retain something of that knowledge. On questions that you aren't really certain about, go with your basic instincts. **Your first impression on how to answer a question is usually correct.**

6. <u>Mark your answers directly on the test booklet</u>. Don't bother trying to fill in the optical scan sheet on the first pass through the test.

Just be very careful not to miss-mark your answers when you eventually transcribe them to the scan sheet.

7. <u>Watch the clock</u>! You have a set amount of time to answer the questions. Don't get bogged down trying to answer a single question at the expense of 10 questions you can more readily answer.

THIS PAGE BLANK

COMPETENCY 1.0 KNOWLEDGE OF THE NATURE OF SCIENCE

Skill 1.1   Analyze processes of scientific inquiry.

Science may be defined as a body of knowledge that is systematically derived from study, observations, and experimentation. Its goal is to identify and establish principles and theories that may be applied to solve problems. *Pseudoscience*, on the other hand, is a belief that is not warranted. There is no scientific methodology or application involved. Some of the more classic examples of pseudoscience include witchcraft, alien encounters, or any topics that are explained by hearsay.

Scientific inquiry starts with observation. After observing, a question is formed, which starts with "why" or "how." To answer these questions, experimentation is necessary. Between observation and experimentation, there are three more important steps. These are: gathering information (or researching about the problem), stating a hypothesis, and designing the experiment.

Designing an experiment involves identifying controls, constants, independent variables and dependent variables. A control or standard is something we compare our results with at the end of the experiment. It is like a reference. Constants are the factors we keep constant in an experiment to get reliable results. Independent variables are factors we change in the experiment. It is important to remember that there should be more constants than variables to obtain reproducible results in an experiment.

Classifying is grouping items according to their similarities. It is important for students to realize relationships and similarity as well as differences to reach a reasonable conclusion in a lab experience.

After the experiment is completed, it is repeated and results are graphically presented. The results are then analyzed and conclusions drawn.

After the conclusion is drawn, the final step is communication. In this age, a lot of emphasis is put on the method of communication. The conclusions must be communicated by clearly describing the information using accurate data, visual presentation (such as bar, line, or pie graphs), tables/charts, diagrams, artwork, and other appropriate media, such as a Power Point presentation. Modern technology must be used whenever it is necessary. The method of communication must be suitable to the audience.

Written communication is as important as oral communication. This is essential for submitting research papers to scientific journals, newspapers, magazines, etc.

Skill 1.2   Evaluate models used in science to explain patterns observed in nature (e.g., rock cycle, heliocentric, geocentric, nitrogen cycle, water cycle).

A **model** is a basic element of scientific inquiry. Many phenomena in science are studied with models. A model is a simplification or representation of a problem that is being studied or predicted. A model is a substitute, but it is similar to what it represents. We use models to describe the solar system, explain how Earth materials are recycled, illustrate the structure of an atom, and more. Physicists use Newton's laws to predict how objects will interact, such as planets and spaceships. In geology, the continental drift model estimates the past positions of continents. At every step of scientific study, models are extensively used. The primary activity of hundreds of thousands of U.S. scientists is to produce new models; these models are presented to the scientific community and the general public in tens of thousands of scientific papers published every year.

Some examples of scientific models:

The **rock cycle** is a model that describes the various complex geologic processes that create, destroy, and modify rocks. The rock cycle model represents the ways in which rocks are continually modified, changing between igneous, sedimentary, and metamorphic, as they move through the cycle. For example, igneous rocks are those created by magma. Igneous rocks exposed at the surface may be broken down by erosion. The resultant sediments may later become lithified, turning into sedimentary rocks. Igneous or sedimentary rocks that are exposed to extreme heat and pressure beneath Earth's crust undergo changes without melting—these are metamorphic rocks. As the rock cycle illustrates, any type of rock can be changed into any other type, if the conditions are right. In this sense, no rocks are truly created or destroyed, since they are all constantly being recycled.

The **heliocentric** model is the one that we currently use to describe our solar system. Heliocentric refers to the fact that in this model, the Sun is at the center. Prior to the development and acceptance of the heliocentric model, people believed the **geocentric** model (Earth at the center) correctly represented the solar system.

The **nitrogen cycle** is a model used to represent the movement of nitrogen through the atmosphere, geosphere, and biosphere. The main processes involved in the nitrogen cycle are nitrogen fixation, nitrogen uptake, nitrogen mineralization, nitrification, and denitrification. Nitrogen fixation refers to the conversion of nitrogen in its gaseous form (by bacteria) to a form useable by plants. Nitrogen uptake occurs when plants absorb nitrogen from the soil, after hit has been "fixed." Nitrogen mineralization refers to the process by which organic nitrogen from decaying plant and animal matter is converted to ammonia and ammonium. Nitrification is the process by which bacteria transform ammonia to nitrite and nitrate, which can be taken up by plants. Lastly, denitrification changes oxidized forms of nitrogen (such as nitrite and nitrate) into dinitrogen (N_2) and nitrous oxide gas.

The **water cycle**, or **hydrologic cycle**, is a model used to represent the cycling of water through the atmosphere, geosphere, hydrosphere, and biosphere. The water cycle models the movement of water between storage areas (such as clouds, lakes, oceans, ice caps, etc.) through processes including evaporation, condensation, precipitation, runoff, groundwater discharge, sublimation, and evapotranspiration.

Skill 1.3   Identify the influences of science and society on each other.

Science and society are closely intertwined. The influence of social and cultural factors on science is profound. In a way, we can say that society has changed the face of science by absorbing scientific innovations. Science has always been a significant part of society. In ancient societies, people did not conceptualize science but took it as a part of their lives. In the modern society, everything has a label and a name, so people are aware of science and other disciplines.

Societies have had trouble accepting science, especially where the science exposed some cultural aspects as myths. A dilemma was created: whether to accept the proven facts provided by scientific investigations or cling to cultural norms. This went on for centuries. It took a long time for societies to accept scientific facts and leave behind some cultural practices, or to modify them. There are two main groups—cultural practices by societies which are scientifically correct and cultural practices which have no scientific foundation (myths and superstitions). A society's progress depends on distinguishing between these two. Some indigenous societies suffered when they were not quick to adjust, since their cultures are very ancient and people found it difficult to accept new challenges and adapt to new changes. At the same time, ancient cultures like the Chinese, Egyptian, Greek, Asian, and Indian were scientifically advanced, as was recorded in their writings.

If we compare science to a volcano, technology is like lava spewing out of the volcano. This was the scenario in the last few centuries in terms of rapid strides in the development of technology. Technology greatly influenced society and culture. At the same time, like a two-way street, science and culture exercised their influence on technology.

Although available, even today some cultures are not using modern technology. Other cultures have so readily adapted to technology that lives are inundated with it. Our lives have become intertwined with technology so much that we utilize the computer, television, microwave, dishwasher, washing machine, cell phone, etc. on a daily basis. Cultures that are not in tune with modern technology are falling behind. It is often argued that to live without technology yields peace of mind, serenity and happiness, but it also results in the loss of valuable opportunities in this age of communication.

Technology has revolutionized education, medicine, communication, and travel. Additionally, technology has provided methods of global to the extent that the planet has seemed to shrink; it is now possible to communicate with almost anyone, anywhere, in a matter of seconds.

Skill 1.4   Analyze the synergistic relationships between basic and applied research, technology, the economy, and the public good.

The relationship among basic and applied research, technology, the economy, and society is such that each is interdependent on the others. Basic research is the starting point in this chain of events. Basic research provides knowledge, which is of two types. The first type of knowledge is theoretical knowledge, giving us the understanding of processes. The second type of knowledge could be applied for the benefit of humanity. Applied research is valuable because it is directly useful to us; it deals with issues like AIDS, Tuberculosis, HPV, Parkinson's Disease, etc. This is important to society because it is useful to the public. Citizens are interested in it and public has its own opinions about the research. As an example, let's look at stem cell research. There are people for and against this controversial piece of research. We are living in the age of technology. We are afraid that we may not be able to function without technology. Such is the relationship of society with technology. The economy, technology and public are inseparable, in that our money, comforts, and modern knowledge are so intertwined with each of these three fields.

This synergistic relationship overlaps some moral and ethical issues. Whatever research is done, public has a right to know it. The economy should not be the guiding force for any piece of research or technology. Clear objectives are critical because the public has a stake in these ventures, especially if they are federally funded. If they are privately funded, the organizations need to remember that they are bound by social ethics and correct practices.

The ultimate goal of any research, technology project, or economic venture must be for the benefit of public.

Skill 1.5   Evaluate the appropriate use of inferences, assumptions, observations, hypotheses, conclusions, laws, and theories.

Inference – the conclusion that something is true in light of something else being or seeming true. An inference can be correct or incorrect.

Assumption – an idea whose truth is taken for granted as fact, even though it may not be. An assumption can be correct or incorrect.

Observation – when one perceives activity and records that activity.

Hypothesis - an unproved theory or educated guess to best explain a phenomena. The validity of a hypothesis may be tested through research.

Conclusion – takes into account observations, data, and previous information to make a logical statement about what has occurred. May also define what steps should be taken next.

Law – an explanation of events that occur with uniformity under the same conditions (laws of nature, law of gravity).

Theory – the formation of principles or relationships which have been verified and accepted. A theory is a proven hypothesis.

Skill 1.6   Analyze scientific data presented in tables, graphs, and diagrams.

When first collected, data are initially organized into tables, spreadsheets, or databases. For example, the table below presents carbon dioxide concentrations taken over many years atop the Mauna Loa Observatory in Hawaii.

Atmospheric CO$_2$ concentrations at Mauna Loa

(CDIAC- Carbon Dioxide Information Analysis Center)

Year	Jan.	Feb.	March	April	May	June	July	Aug.	Sept.	Oct.	Nov.	Dec.	Annual
1958	--	--	315.71	317.45	317.50	--	315.86	314.93	313.19	--	313.34	314.67	--
1959	315.58	316.47	316.65	317.71	318.29	318.16	316.55	314.80	313.84	313.34	314.81	315.59	315.98
1960	316.43	316.97	317.58	319.03	320.03	319.59	318.18	315.91	314.16	313.83	315.00	316.19	316.91
1961	316.89	317.70	318.54	319.48	320.58	319.78	318.58	316.79	314.99	315.31	316.10	317.01	317.65
1962	317.94	318.56	319.69	320.58	321.01	320.61	319.61	317.40	316.26	315.42	316.69	317.69	318.45
1963	318.74	319.08	319.86	321.39	322.24	321.47	319.74	317.77	316.21	315.99	317.07	318.36	318.99
1964	319.57	--	--	--	322.23	321.89	320.44	318.70	316.70	316.87	317.68	318.71	--
1965	319.44	320.44	320.89	322.13	322.16	321.87	321.21	318.87	317.81	317.30	318.87	319.42	320.03
1966	320.62	321.59	322.39	323.70	324.07	323.75	322.40	320.37	318.64	318.10	319.79	321.03	321.37
1967	322.33	322.50	323.04	324.42	325.00	324.09	322.55	320.92	319.26	319.39	320.72	321.96	322.18
1968	322.57	323.15	323.89	325.02	325.57	325.36	324.14	322.11	320.33	320.25	321.32	322.90	323.05
1969	324.00	324.42	325.64	326.66	327.38	326.70	325.89	323.67	322.38	321.78	322.85	324.12	324.62
1970	325.06	325.98	326.93	328.13	328.07	327.66	326.35	324.69	323.10	323.07	324.01	325.13	325.68
1971	326.17	326.68	327.18	327.78	328.92	328.57	327.37	325.43	323.36	323.56	324.80	326.01	326.32
1972	326.77	327.63	327.75	329.72	330.07	329.09	328.05	326.32	324.84	325.20	326.50	327.55	327.46
1973	328.54	329.56	330.30	331.50	332.48	332.07	330.87	329.31	327.51	327.18	328.16	328.64	329.68
1974	329.35	330.71	331.48	332.65	333.09	332.25	331.18	329.40	327.44	327.37	328.46	329.58	330.25
1975	330.40	331.41	332.04	333.31	333.96	333.59	331.91	330.06	328.56	328.34	329.49	330.76	331.15
1976	331.74	332.56	333.50	334.58	334.87	334.34	333.05	330.94	329.30	328.94	330.31	331.68	332.15
1977	332.92	333.42	334.70	336.07	336.74	336.27	334.93	332.75	331.58	331.16	332.40	333.85	333.90
1978	334.97	335.39	336.64	337.76	338.01	337.89	336.54	334.68	332.76	332.54	333.92	334.95	335.50
1979	336.23	336.76	337.96	338.89	339.47	339.29	337.73	336.09	333.91	333.86	335.29	336.73	336.85
1980	338.01	338.36	340.08	340.77	341.46	341.17	339.56	337.60	335.88	336.01	337.10	338.21	338.69
1981	339.23	340.47	341.38	342.51	342.91	342.25	340.49	338.43	336.69	336.85	338.36	339.61	339.93
1982	340.75	341.61	342.70	343.56	344.13	343.35	342.06	339.82	337.97	337.86	339.26	340.49	341.13
1983	341.37	342.52	343.10	344.94	345.75	345.32	343.99	342.39	339.86	339.99	341.16	342.99	342.78
1984	343.70	344.51	345.28	347.08	347.43	346.79	345.40	343.28	341.07	341.35	342.98	344.22	344.42
1985	344.97	346.00	347.43	348.35	348.93	348.25	346.56	344.69	343.09	342.80	344.24	345.56	345.90
1986	346.29	346.96	347.86	349.55	350.21	349.54	347.94	345.91	344.86	344.17	345.66	346.90	347.15
1987	348.02	348.47	349.42	350.99	351.84	351.25	349.52	348.10	346.44	346.36	347.81	348.96	348.93
1988	350.43	351.72	352.22	353.59	354.22	353.79	352.39	350.44	348.72	348.88	350.07	351.34	351.48
1989	352.76	353.07	353.68	355.42	355.67	355.13	353.90	351.67	349.80	349.99	351.30	352.53	352.91
1990	353.66	354.70	355.39	356.20	357.16	356.22	354.82	352.91	350.96	351.18	352.83	354.21	354.19
1991	354.72	355.75	357.16	358.60	359.34	358.24	356.17	354.03	352.16	352.21	353.75	354.99	355.59
1992	355.98	356.72	357.81	359.15	359.66	359.25	357.03	355.00	353.01	353.31	354.16	355.40	356.37
1993	356.70	357.16	358.38	359.46	360.28	359.60	357.57	355.52	353.70	353.98	355.33	356.80	357.04
1994	358.36	358.91	359.97	361.26	361.68	360.95	359.55	357.49	355.84	355.99	357.58	359.04	358.88
1995	359.96	361.00	361.64	363.45	363.79	363.26	361.90	359.46	358.06	357.75	359.56	360.70	360.88
1996	362.05	363.25	364.03	364.72	365.41	364.97	363.65	361.49	359.46	359.60	360.76	362.33	362.64
1997	363.18	364.00	364.57	366.35	366.79	365.62	364.47	362.51	360.19	360.77	362.43	364.28	363.76
1998	365.32	366.15	367.31	368.61	369.30	368.87	367.64	365.77	363.90	364.23	365.46	366.97	366.63
1999	368.15	368.86	369.58	371.12	370.97	370.33	369.25	366.91	364.60	365.09	366.63	367.96	368.29
2000	369.08	369.40	370.45	371.59	371.75	371.62	370.04	368.04	366.54	366.63	368.20	369.43	369.40
2001	370.17	371.39	372.00	372.75	373.88	373.17	371.48	369.42	367.83	367.96	369.55	371.10	370.89
2002	372.29	372.94	373.38	374.71	375.40	375.26	373.87	371.35	370.57	370.10	371.93	373.63	372.95

Looking at this table of data in various ways we can make several observations, with the help of a calculator:

- **Data completeness** – There are some gaps in the data between 1958 and 1964. From 1965 on, observations of CO_2 levels in the atmosphere have been made consistently every month.

- **Seasonal effects** – Looking across the rows of data, we can identify seasonal trends within years. For example, we can see that the highest concentrations tend to be in April, May, and June and the lowest concentrations tend to be in September and October. The difference appears to be about 4-5 ppm.

- **Long term trends** – Looking down the columns of data, we can evaluate long-term trends over the years shown. In every month, concentrations of CO_2 have risen approximately 58 ppm over 45 years, or about 1.3 ppm/yr.

While these trends can be observed using tables, it is much easier when the data are then compiled into graphs or charts. Graphs help scientists visualize and interpret variations and patterns in data. The following is the same set of data as a line graph. This is a famous graph called the Keeling Curve (courtesy NASA).

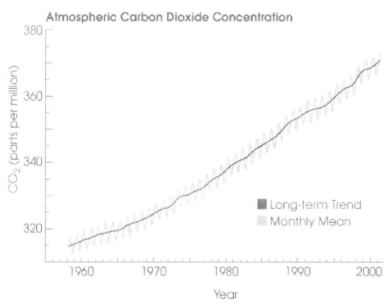

In the graph, the x-axis represents time in units of years and the y-axis represents CO_2 concentration in units of parts per million (ppm). The best fit line (solid dark line) shows the trend in CO_2 concentration during the time period shown. This steady upward-sloping line indicates an overall trend of increasing CO_2 concentration between 1958 and 2002. The light blue line, which indicates monthly mean CO_2 levels, shows the periodic variation in CO_2 concentrations during each year. Either the table or the graph can be used to predict future trends in the data.

Example: If CO_2 emission trends continue roughly as they have over the last 40 years, what will be the estimated CO_2 concentration in the atmosphere in 2020?

Solution: The average concentration of CO_2 in 2002 is listed in the table in the right-hand column, and is 372.95 ppm. 18 yrs multiplied by an average increase of about 1.3 ppm/yr = 23.4 ppm increase by 2020, for a total concentration of about 396.4 ppm CO_2.

Skill 1.7 **Differentiate between qualitative and quantitative data in experimental, observational, and modeling methods of research.**

Quantitative is derived from quantity (numerical, precise) and qualitative (impressive) is derived from quality. Qualitative and quantitative data can be compared and differentiated as follows:

1. Assumptions:
In quantitative experimentation, the method is of primary importance. Variables are identified and relationships are measured. In qualitative experimentation, subject matter is of prime importance. Variables are complex, not clearly established, and are interwoven and difficult to measure.

2. Purpose:
In quantitative data, data is generalized, with prediction and casual explanation. In qualitative data, there is contextualization, interpretation, and understanding of perspectives.

3. Approach:
Quantitative research begins with hypotheses and theories. Experiments are conducted using instruments and deduction. Components are analyzed, data are reduced to indices and abstract language is used in conclusion. Qualitative research ends with hypotheses and theories. The researcher is the instrument and the reasoning is inductive. There is minor use of numerical indices and the write up is descriptive.

4. Role of the researcher:
The quantitative researcher is detached and impartial and is objective in carrying out the research. The qualitative researcher is partial and personally involved and has empathetic understanding.

Skill 1.8 **Apply state statutes and national guidelines regarding laboratory safety, hazardous materials, experimentation, and the use of organisms in the classroom.**

Safety in the science classroom and laboratory is of paramount importance to the science educator. The following is a general summary of the types of safety equipment that should be made available within a given school system as well as general locations where the protective equipment or devices should be maintained and used. Please note that this is only a partial list and that your school system should be reviewed for unique and site-specific hazards at each facility.

The key to maintaining a safe learning environment is through proactive training and regular in-service updates for all staff and students who utilize the science laboratory. Proactive training should include how to identify potential hazards, evaluate potential hazards, and how to prevent or respond to hazards. The following types of training should be considered:

a) Right to Know (OSHA training on the importance and benefits of properly recognizing and safely working with hazardous materials) along with some basic chemical hygiene as well as how to read and understand material safety data sheets,

b) instruction in how to use a fire extinguisher,

c) instruction in how to use a chemical fume hood,

d) general guidance in when and how to use personal protective equipment (e.g. safety glasses or gloves), and

e) instruction in how to monitor activities for potential impacts on indoor air quality.

It is also important for the instructor to utilize **Material Data Safety Sheets**. Maintain a copy of the material safety data sheet for every item in your chemical inventory. This information will assist you in determining how to store and handle your materials by outlining the health and safety hazards posed by the substance. In most cases the manufacturer will provide recommendations with regard to protective equipment, ventilation and storage practices. This information should be your first guide when considering the use of a new material.

Frequent monitoring and in-service training on all equipment, materials, and procedures will help to ensure a safe and orderly laboratory environment. It will also provide everyone who uses the laboratory the safety fundamentals necessary to discern a safety hazard and to respond appropriately.

With appropriate planning and training, the maintenance of safe practices and procedures in areas of science instruction becomes integrated with the procedures for instruction and laboratory investigation. Safety procedures should be taught early and emphasized often to maintain a high level of safety awareness.

Safety Equipment

- Keep appropriate safety equipment on hand, including an emergency shower, eye-wash station, fume hood, fire blankets, and fire extinguisher. All students and teacher(s) should have and wear safety goggles and protective aprons when working in the lab.

- Ensure proper eye protection devices are worn by everyone engaged in supervising, observing, or conducting science activities involving potential hazards to the eye.

- Provide protective rubber or latex gloves for students when they dissect laboratory specimens.

- Use heat-safety items such as safety tongs, mittens, and aprons when handling either cold or hot materials.

- Use safety shields or screens whenever there is potential danger that an explosion or implosion might occur.

- Keep a bucket of 90 percent sand and 10 percent vermicullite or kitty litter (dried bentonite particles) in all rooms in which chemicals are handled or stored. The bucket must be properly labeled and have a lid that prevents other debris from contaminating the contents.

Teaching Procedures

- Set a good example when demonstrating experiments by modeling safety techniques such as wearing aprons and goggles.

- Help students develop a positive attitude toward safety. Students should not fear doing experiments or using reagents or equipment, but they should respect them as potential hazards.

- Always demonstrate procedures before allowing students to begin the activity. Look for possible hazards and alert students to potential dangers.

- Explain and post safety instructions each time you conduct an experiment.

- Maintain constant supervision of student activities. Never allow students to perform unauthorized experiments or conduct experiments in the laboratory alone.

- Protect all laboratory animals and ensure that they are treated humanely.

- Remind students that many plants have poisonous parts and should be handled with care.

- For safety, consider the National Science Teachers Association's recommendation to limit science classes to 24 or fewer students.

Student Safety Tips

- Read lab materials in advance. Note all cautions (written and oral).

- Never assume an experiment is safe just because it is in print.

- Do not eat or drink in the laboratory.

- Keep personal items off of the lab benches.

- Restrain long hair and loose clothing. Wear laboratory aprons when appropriate.

- Avoid all rough play and mischief in science classrooms or labs.

- Wear closed-toed shoes when conducting experiments.

- Never use mouth suction when filling pipettes with chemical reagents.

- Never force rubber stoppers into glass tubing.

- Avoid transferring chemicals to your face, hands, or other areas of exposed skin.

- Thoroughly clean all work surfaces and equipment after each use.

- Make certain all hot plates and burners are turned off before leaving the laboratory.

Lab Environment

- Place smoke, carbon monoxide, and heat detectors in laboratories and storerooms.

- Ensure that all new laboratories have two unobstructed exits. Consider adding additional exits to rooms with only one door.

- Frequently inspect a laboratory's electrical, gas, and water systems.

- Install ground fault circuit interrupters (GFCI outlets) at all electrical outlets in science laboratories.

- Install a single central shut-off for gas, electricity, and water for all the laboratories in the school, especially if your school is in an earthquake zone.

- Maintain Material Safety Data Sheets (MSDS) on all school chemicals and an inventory of all science equipment.

- Conduct frequent laboratory inspections and an annual, verified safety check of each laboratory.

In addition to the safety laws set forth by the government for equipment necessary to the lab, OSHA (Occupational Safety and Health Administration) has helped to make environments safer by instituting signs that are bilingual. These signs use pictures rather than/in addition to words and feature eye-catching colors. Some of the best known examples are exit, restrooms, and handicap accessible.

Of particular importance to laboratories are diamond safety signs, prohibitive signs, and triangle danger signs. Each sign encloses a descriptive picture.

Skill 1.9   Differentiate between the various roles of communication in the development of scientific ideas (e.g., collaboration, peer review, scientific debate).

The development of scientific ideas relies upon communication among scientists. In addition to the use of the scientific method (hypothesis formation and subsequent testing), the acceptance of new scientific information requires that other members of the scientific world evaluate new ideas and findings. Often scientists will **collaborate** when working on new ideas. Input from several different scientists, especially if from different (but related) disciplines, can greatly enhance the development of new ideas. **Peer review** is another integral part of the development of scientific ideas. The peer review process means that before a scientific paper is published, it is scrutinized by independent qualified experts to ensure the validity and soundness of the ideas in the paper. This peer review process ensures that only high-quality research is published. **Scientific debate** refers to the process by which scientists argue about the validity of new hypotheses or ideas. Many new scientific ideas are at first subject to scrutiny, and are not always accepted. When scientists debate the validity of new claims, it helps ensure that only the strongest research and most robust ideas become accepted as fact.

Skill 1.10   Distinguish between accuracy, precision, systematic error, and random error, using significant figures appropriately.

Accuracy and Precision

Accuracy is the degree of conformity of a measured, calculated quantity to its actual (true) value. **Precision**, also called reproducibility or repeatability, is the degree to which further measurements or calculations will show the same or similar results.

Accuracy is the degree of veracity while precision is the degree of reproducibility. The best analogy to explain accuracy and precision is the target comparison.

Repeated measurements are compared to arrows that are fired at a target. Accuracy describes the closeness of arrows to the bull's eye at the target center. Arrows that strike closer to the bull's eye are considered more accurate. A group of arrows that may or may not be near the bull's eye, but are near one another, represent precision.

Systematic and Random Error

All experimental uncertainty is due to either random errors or systematic errors.

Random errors are statistical fluctuations in the measured data due to the precision limitations of the measurement device. Random errors usually result from the experimenter's inability to take the same measurement in exactly the same way to acquire exactly the same number.

Systematic errors, by contrast, are reproducible inaccuracies that are consistently in the same direction. Systematic errors are often due to a problem that persists throughout the entire experiment, and are usually caused by an instrumental or human error.

Significant Figures

Significant figures or **significant digits** are the digits indicating the precision of a measurement. There is uncertainty in the last digit only.

Example: You measure an object with a ruler marked in millimeters. The reading on the ruler is found to be about 2/3 of the way between 12 and 13 mm. What value should be recorded for its length?

Solution: Recording 13 mm does not give all the information that you found. Recording 12 $\frac{2}{3}$ mm implies that an exact ratio was determined. Recording 12.666 mm gives more information than you found. A value of 12.7 mm or 12.6 mm should be recorded because there is uncertainty only in the last digit.

There are five rules for determining the **number of significant digits** in a quantity:

1) All nonzero digits are significant and all zeros between nonzero digits are significant.
   Example: 4.521 and 7002 both have four significant digits.
2) Zeros to the left of the first nonzero digit are not significant.
   Example: 0.0002 contains one significant digit.
3) Zeros to the right of a non-zero digit and the decimal point are significant.
   Example: 32.500 contains five significant figures.
4) The significance of numbers ending in zeros that are not to the right of the decimal point can be unclear, so this situation should be avoided by using scientific notation or a different decimal prefix. Sometimes a decimal point is used as a placeholder to indicate the units-digit is significant. A word like "thousand" or "million" may be used in informal contexts to indicate that the remaining digits are not significant.

   Example: 12000 m would be considered to have five significant digits by many scientists, but in the sentence, "The distance is between 11000 m and 12000 m," it almost certainly has only two. "12 thousand meters" only has two significant digits, but 12000.0 m has five, as indicated by the decimal point. The value should be represented as 1.2×10^4 m (or 1.2000×10^4 m). The best alternative would be to use 12 km or 12.000 km.

Exact numbers have no uncertainty and contain an infinite number of significant digits. These relationships are **definitions**. They are not measurements.

Example: There are exactly 1000 L in one cubic meter.

There are two rules for **rounding off significant digits**:

1) If the leftmost digit to be removed is a four or less, then round down. The last remaining digit stays as it was.

   Example: Round 43.4 g to two significant digits. Answer: 43 g.

2) If the leftmost digit to be removed is a five or more, then round up. The last remaining digit increases by one.

   Example: Round 6.772 g to two significant digits. Answer: 6.8 g.

Skill 1.11   Evaluate variables and affected outcomes for appropriate experimental designs with minimum bias.

Designing an experiment properly is critical because the success of the experiment depends on it. Before designing an experiment, one must identify the elements of an experiment.

1. **Control/standard**: A control is something the results of an experiment are compared against. Without this, we have no clue of the significance of the data obtained in an experiment.
2. **Constants**: An experiment needs to have multiple constants for better results. Many factors should be kept constant in an experiment. The reliability of the data/results depends to a greater extent on the number of constants. So, it is very important to identify all the possible constants in an experiment, which then make for a well-controlled experiment.
3. **Independent variables**: These are the variables we have the power to change. It is entirely at our discretion to choose the independent variables. These factors are going to influence the outcome of the experiment. One should remember that the number of independent variables must be limited to a maximum of four, otherwise the experiment gets complicated and the data may not be reliable.
4. **Dependent variable**: This is the factor that will be measured in an experiment. It is called dependent variable since its outcome is dependent on the independent variables.

After the experiment is conducted, it is of utmost importance to repeat the experiment at least twice to obtain reliable data, which will then be analyzed and conclusions drawn.

Inferring is a very important skill since it interprets the results and facilitates the researcher/scientist to draw logical conclusions.

Lastly, there is another important element to the experiment. The conclusions drawn must be communicated orally, and in written form for the benefit of furthering knowledge and sharing with the community to enlighten and educate it scientifically. This will help the society to become scientifically literate.

Bias

Scientific research can be biased in the choice of what data to consider, in the reporting or recording of the data, and/or in how the data are interpreted. The scientist's emphasis may be influenced by his/her nationality, sex, ethnic origin, age, or political convictions. For example, when studying a group of animals, male scientists may focus on the social behavior of the males and typically male characteristics.

Although bias related to the investigator, the sample, the method, or the instrument may not be completely avoidable in every case, it is important to know the possible sources of bias and how bias could affect the evidence. Moreover, scientists need to be attentive to possible bias in their own work as well as that of other scientists.

Objectivity may not always be attained. However, one precaution that may be taken to guard against undetected bias is to have many different investigators or groups of investigators working on a project. By different, it is meant that the groups are made up of various nationalities, ethnic origins, ages, and political convictions and composed of both males and females. It is also important to note one's aspirations, and to make sure to be truthful to the data, even when grants, promotions, and notoriety are at risk.

Skill 1.12   Identify the equipment Earth and space scientists use to gather, analyze, and interpret data in field and laboratory investigations.

(See Skill 12.2 for a detailed discussion of equipment used by space scientists.)

From hand lenses to supercomputers, Earth and space scientists use a vast array of equipment to gather, analyze, and interpret data. Many geologists use tools including hand lenses, rock hammers, field notebooks, compasses, GPS devices, maps, and cameras to collect samples and make observations in the field.

Below is a description of some specific tools:

Computer technology has greatly improved the collection and interpretation of scientific data. Molecular findings have been enhanced through the use of computer images. Technology has revolutionized access to data via the Internet and shared databases. The manipulation of data is enhanced by sophisticated software capabilities. Computers are used to model phenomena within Earth and in outer space. Practically every subfield of Earth and space science is enhanced by the use of computer technology.

Satellites have many uses and play an important role in Earth and space investigations. They can be used to observe Earth's surface features from space, study Earth's upper atmosphere, examine celestial objects, aid in navigation, and more.

Radar and sonar technology allow Earth scientists to map both surface and subsurface features on Earth and other celestial bodies. Sonar also allows for mapping of the ocean floor.

Seismographs record vibrations in Earth and allow scientists to measure earthquake activity.

Tiltmeters are used to measure small changes in the orientation or tilt of the ground surface or of a structure. In Earth science, tiltmeters are useful for monitoring changes in the ground surface in seismically or volcanically active areas.

Mass spectrometers are machines that sort atoms according to weight. The information provided by mass spectrometers can be used for everything from dating rocks and fossils to analyzing ancient climates.

X-ray diffraction can be used to determine the crystalline structure, chemical composition, and physical properties of a sample of geologic material.

Scanning electron microscopes can be used to determine the surface structure of a sample, as well as reveal its composition.

COMPETENCY 2.0   **KNOWLEDGE OF THE COMPOSITION, CHARACTERISTICS, AND STRUCTURE OF EARTH**

Skill 2.1   **Identify the characteristics of Earth's layers and the methods used to investigate Earth's interior.**

Layering by Physical Properties

Lithosphere: The term Lithosphere is Greek for "rock layer." Comprised of the crust and uppermost part of the mantle, the lithosphere consists of cool, rigid, and brittle materials. Most earthquakes originate in the lithosphere. Because it is close to the surface, both temperature and pressure are relatively low in comparison to the other layers.

Asthenosphere: This layer is the semi-plastic molten rock material located directly below the lithosphere. At the base of the asthenosphere, the mantle again becomes more rigid and less plastic, and it remains in that rigid state all the way to the core.

Transition zone: The transition zone is characterized by a sudden increase in density. This zone marks the change from the weaker asthenosphere to the rigid lower mantle.

Mesosphere: The lower mantle is rigid, hard, and brittle.

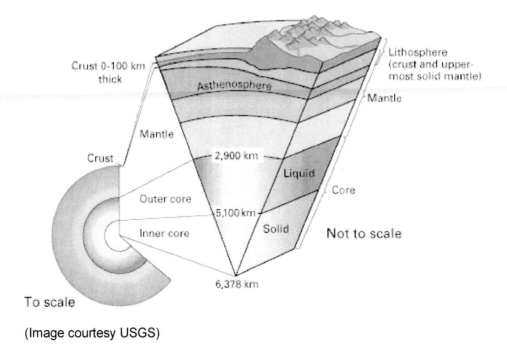

(Image courtesy USGS)

Layering by Chemical Composition

Crust: The crust is Earth's thin, rocky outer shell. There are two types of crust:
- Oceanic crust is thin and dense. Made of basalt.
- Continental crust is thicker and much less dense than oceanic crust. Made of a variety of rock types.

Mantle: The mantle is a thick layer of hot, solid rock. It comprises about 2/3 of the mass of Earth and is about 2900 km thick.

Core: The core is found at the center of Earth, and is an iron-nickel alloy. It has two distinct regions:
- The outer core is a liquid layer.
- The inner core is solid.

Methods to Investigate Earth's Interior

Seismic tomography uses seismic waves to develop three-dimensional views of Earth. Each time there is an earthquake, waves travel through Earth in all directions and are recorded by seismographs around the world. Scientists know the precise time the waves should reach any given seismograph; however, some waves arrive either before or after the predicted time. This is because the waves speed up when traveling through colder, more rigid regions, and slow down when they are in warmer, less rigid regions. Using earthquake data from around the world, scientists are able to create cross sections of Earth's interior based on the travel times of seismic waves. Using a series of cross sections, they can then create a 3D image.

Seismic reflection relies on sound waves that are bounced off boundaries between different types of rocks, revealing the location and depth of these boundaries. This method is good for exploring structures deep in the crust.

Seismic refraction differs from seismic reflection in that it relies on sound waves that, rather than bouncing back to the surface, change direction and a geologic boundary and travel along it before returning to the surface. Seismic refraction is better suited to exploring the crust at shallower depths (less than 100 feet below ground).

Skill 2.2   Identify common rocks and minerals based on their physical and chemical properties.

Minerals

A **mineral** is a naturally occurring inorganic solid with a well-defined chemical composition and a crystalline structure.

Some minerals are single elements. An example of this is a diamond, which is solely carbon (C). Some minerals are simple combinations of atoms. Examples of this are halite (NaCl) and pyrite (FeS_2). Other minerals are complex combinations of atoms. An example of this is tourmaline: (Na,Ca) (Mg,Li,Al,Fe^{2+},Fe^{3+})$_3$ (Al,Mg,Cr)$_6$ B$_3$ Si$_6$ (OH,O,F)$_4$

Crystalline structure, form or shape—not chemical composition—is the key defining factor in identifying minerals. Crystalline structure is defined as the most efficient arrangement of atoms that form a crystal shape.

Minerals are arranged in specific patterns based on their elemental composition. For example, halite (NaCl) forms into cube shapes, while a diamond's structure is a complex latticework of diamond shapes.

Polymorphism - Two minerals with identical chemical compositions, but entirely different crystalline structures. For instance, diamonds and graphite are identical in chemical composition- both are pure carbon (C)- but their crystalline forms are radically different. Diamonds have an incredibly complex structured framework, while graphite is striated in flat sheets. Crystalline structure defines a mineral's properties, and these properties are the primary indicators used to identify a specific mineral.

With literally thousands of different minerals, the task of identification can seem daunting. However, determining the type of mineral is also very important. Some minerals are often found together, and the presence of one may indicate the presence of another, more commercially valuable mineral.

Primary Identifying Properties

Crystal habit: the shape of the mineral. Some minerals possess distinctive shapes.

Cleavage: how the mineral breaks under pressure. Most minerals have a tendency to break in a preferred direction along smooth surfaces. Where the atoms connect, it forms a weak point. For example, mica is resistant to breaking but peels quite easily. Not all minerals have cleavage. Instead, some fracture. Example: Quartz shatters like glass.

Hardness: how hard the mineral is. Hardness is based upon the arrangement of atoms within the crystalline structure. Hardness is graded from 1 to 10, using Mohs Scale of Hardness.

Mohs Scale of Hardness

1. Talc
2. Gypsum
3. Calcite
4. Fluorite
5. Apatite
6. Orthoclase
7. Quartz
8. Topaz
9. Corundum
10. Diamond

General classification is acceptable based on the **scratch test**.

Soft: Able to be scratched with a fingernail.
Hard: Able to scratch glass with the mineral.
Medium: not able to be scratched with a fingernail, nor able to scratch glass with the mineral.

Specific gravity: the ratio of the mineral's weight to water. Because the weight of the mineral is based upon the arrangement of the atoms, minerals will vary in specific gravity. (e.g. water = 1, but rock = 2.65.)

Color: the color of the mineral in solid form. Although some minerals, such as Sulfur, are distinctly colored- always some shade of yellow- it's relatively common to find color variations within the same mineral. As a result, identifying minerals using color exclusively can easily lead to misidentification.

Streak: the color of the mineral in powdered form. Some minerals leave a distinctive color streak when the mineral is scratched across a streak plate (a piece of unglazed porcelain).

Additional (Secondary) Identifying Properties

Luster: the surface appearance of the mineral.
Examples of luster are pearly, waxy, shiny, dull, earthy, and glassy.

Magnetism: inherent magnetic qualities.
Example: magnetite=yes, quartz=no.

Fluorescence: Some minerals glow under a black light.
Example: lapis lazuli.

Reaction to acid: Some minerals have a distinctive reaction when exposed to acids. For example: Any mineral with calcium carbonate ($CaCO_3$) will fizz when diluted hydrochloric acid (HCl) is dropped on it.

Striations: distinctive marks on the surface of the mineral. These marks are usually parallel lines on the mineral surface. For example, feldspar is often heavily striated.

Taste: Some minerals have a distinctive taste.
Example: halite (NaCl) (more commonly known as table salt)

Rocks

A **rock** is a solid comprised of one or more minerals.

There are three main categories of rocks: igneous, metamorphic and sedimentary.

Igneous rocks are rocks that are formed from a melt, which is created by extreme pressure and temperature deep below the surface of Earth.

Material in a melt is referred to as either:
Magma: melted rock material below ground, or
Lava: melted rock material above ground

As lava cools and solidifies, minerals settle out in combinations based on their respective densities.

Igneous rocks generally appear to have little layering, and an abundance of black, white, gray, and/or pink minerals. Some may look like solidified lava. An example of an igneous rock is **granite**.

Metamorphic rocks are rocks that have undergone a change, or metamorphosis. The change is caused by heat and/or pressure. The degree of metamorphism depends on the magnitude of the heat and/or pressure applied. In this process, the rock doesn't melt; it is simple changed into a new substance. Example: Granite (an igneous rock), can become gneiss (a metamorphic rock).

Metamorphic rocks are classified by texture (appearance). They are either foliated or non-foliated.

Foliated rocks have a banded (striped) appearance to the naked eye. Foliation usually results from regional metamorphism. This classification is further sub-classified by the degree of foliation.

Some examples of foliated rocks are:

Gneiss: Very obvious striped banding.

Schist: "Flaky" appearance. Tends to be shiny (like glitter stuck to the rock or the sheen observed on fish scales).

Slate: "Slaty" cleavage with a slight sheen. Slate looks like shale but does not have a "muddy" appearance, and the edges appear "peelable" at the cleavage. Harder than shale, slate "clinks" when struck. Shale "clunks" when struck.

Non-foliated rocks have no foliation. Examples: quartzite and marble.

Sedimentary rocks are rocks that form from sediments that harden solid rock.

Classification of sedimentary rocks is based upon the way the rock was formed.

Clastic sedimentary rocks are composed of lithified sediments (fragmental), which have undergone compaction/dessification or cementation.

Conglomerates are comprised of large (bigger than sand), rounded particles. They look like a pile of pebbles stuck together.

Breccia is made up of large (bigger than sand), angular particles stuck together. The pieces have sharp edges and sides.

Sandstone is made up of sand-sized particles. The feel and size is dependent on the size of the sand dune that it came from.

Shale: Smaller than sand-sized particles. Particles are the size of clay and/or silt grains. Grains are very fine and can't be seen with the naked eye.

Conglomerate, breccia and sandstone are formed by cementation. Shale is formed by compaction/dessification.

Bioclastic or organic sedimentary rocks are formed from the remains of once-living organisms, usually of marine origin.

Coquina is composed of large shell fragments cemented together. Very easy to identify, coquina was a prized building material in the early settler days. Example: Old Spanish forts in Fort Lauderdale, Florida.

Fossiliferous limestone is composed of calcium carbonate or carbonate materials. Fossils are evident, often from reef material.

Chalk is composed of microscopic calcium carbonate shells. Accumulations can get quite thick. Example: The White Cliffs of Dover in England are Chalk deposits measuring 2000 ft in depth.

Chert is made of microscopic silica shells.

Non-clastic or chemical sedimentary rocks precipitated out of a solution. This is a very slow process, as the rock is formed drop-by-drop. Limestone is an example of a chemical sedimentary rock.

A **geode** occurs when silica is collected inside a cavity in other rocks.

Agate refers to banded silicate materials with light and dark colors.

Skill 2.3   Distinguish between igneous, metamorphic, and sedimentary rocks.

(See also Skill 2.2)

Igneous Rocks

Igneous rocks form from the cooling and crystallization of a rock melt.

Melt: the overall collective term used to describe molten and semi-molten rock material in Earth. The melt is due to the heat present in Earth and this heat is derived from two sources: the decay of radioactive elements and frictional forces and pressure within Earth. As you go deeper into Earth, the temperature increases. The various heat layers are collectively referred to as the **geothermal gradient**.

Other forces can aid or hinder the melt.

Pressure: Rock stays solid longer if it is under pressure.

Presence of water: Dependent on the pressure, the presence of water can delay or accelerate the melt process.

As rock materials move within Earth, rocks in a liquid state move upward, seeking cracks in solid rock, and rocks in a solid state move downward.

Liquid rock slowly cools as it moves upwards. The upward movement can cause enough pressure and stress to move and/or fracture the solid rock.

Crystallization

Magma is rich in chemicals. As it cools, chemicals combine to form distinct mineral structures.

As minerals form, they either settle to the bottom of the magma well, or continue to react and form a richer magma.

Bowen's reaction series is used to predict the order in which minerals solidify out of a melt. These predictions are primarily based on the heat of the magma.

Lavas on the surface have a temperature of around 2000 °F. By comparison, magma-cooling underground can take millions of years because of the extremely high temperatures present below Earth's surface.

Cooling Rates

Slow cooling: forms very large crystals of minerals in the rock. Very large grains are prominent in the rock. Example: granite.

Quick cooling: This allows less time for the crystal to cool and form. It results in smaller- sometimes microscopic- crystals. Example: basalt.

Squelching (instant cooling): This cooling occurs almost instantaneously when lava flows into the ocean or is thrown into the air by an eruption. No crystals form and the rocks usually have a glassy appearance. Example: obsidian.

The cooling rate of the igneous rock is very important because it produces a distinct texture that is a key factor in its identification.

Textural Results

Phaneritic: Igneous rock with mineral grains large enough to be seen with the naked eye. Grain size caused by slow cooling.

Aphanitic: Igneous rock with mineral crystals present, but the crystals are often too small to be seen without the aid of a microscope. Grain size caused by quick cooling.

Categories of Igneous Rocks

Extrusive: Igneous rocks that cool on or near Earth's surface. Characterized by aphanitic or glassy textures.

Intrusive: Igneous rocks that cool deep within Earth. Characterized by phaneritic texture.

Intrusive rocks never reach the surface during the cooling process. Instead, they are exposed after millions of years of weathering. Examples: Stone Mountain, GA, or Half Dome, in Yosemite National Park

Glassy texture: no detectable mineral crystals present. Caused by squelching (instant cooling).

Porphyritic: some large mineral crystals within an aphanitic or glassy ground mass (background). The background is also known as the **matrix** and presents a checkerboard texture. The magma cooled slowly, forming large grains, but before the magma was fully developed, it erupted upward through cracks, cooled quickly, and other minerals formed smaller crystals. Example: diamond head in Hawaii is composed of volcanic basalt with large olivine crystals.

Metamorphic Rocks

Metamorphism: changing a pre-existing rock into a new rock by heat and or pressure. Metamorphism is a process that is similar to that of putting a clay pot into a kiln. The clay doesn't melt, but a solid-state chemical reaction occurs that causes a change.

The chemical bonds of adjoining atoms breakdown and allow the atoms to rearrange themselves, producing a substance with new properties.

Single Mineral Metamorphism

If the pre-existing rock is composed primarily of only one mineral, the metamorphic result is a rock with the same composition, but the crystal grains are larger and interlocked. For example, sandstone is a cementation of silica. Under metamorphosis, the grains become larger and are fused together to form quartzite. There are major differences in appearance and properties. Quartzite appears crystalline with very large crystals and is very hard.

Another example: Metamorphism causes limestone to become marble. Limestone can be cut and used as building material, but it resists polishing, restricting its use as a decorative stone. Marble, on the other hand, can be polished and utilized as a very strong and decorative building material.

Multiple Mineral Metamorphism

If the pre-existing rock is composed of more than one mineral, then pre-existing minerals may align to give a new appearance, or recombination can occur within the rock, producing entirely new minerals.

An example of this is the metamorphic change of granite. It retains the same mineral composition but becomes gneiss, ending up with the materials aligned, giving it a striped appearance. Likewise, garnet is a recombination of multiple minerals and is formed only by metamorphism.

Temperature and/or pressure can cause metamorphism. The metamorphic effect may produce a change in the chemical and physical properties and/or appearance of the rock.

Types of Metamorphism

Contact metamorphosis: This requires the presence of a nearby magma chamber. The closer the heat source, the more metamorphosis that takes place. Key ingredient is temperature. This is a **localized effect** due to the presence of a magma chamber. Effect is measured in tens to hundreds of yards.

Rocks formed during contact metamorphism tend not to become foliated (striped).

Regional metamorphism: This type of metamorphism is produced by the tectonic movement (drift) of continental plates.

Continental drift exerts enormous pressures at the edges of the plate abutments. Rocks are deformed into a semi-plastic state and the atomic bonds are broken. The pressures involved cause the rocks to reform without breaking.

An analogy for this type of metamorphism is that of chocolate chip cookies fresh and hot from the oven. Under pressure, they tend to bend rather than break. In the case of rock material, pressure compression causes the material to fold.

Regional metamorphism has a widespread effect measured in 10's to 100's of miles. Example: The Appalachian Mountains have abundant metamorphic material because the mountains were the result of 3 past collisions between the North American and African plates.

In regional metamorphism the end result are deformed rocks that are highly foliated.

Migrating Fluids – (Also called Metasomatism or Hydrothermal Alteration):
Formed by groundwater heated by a magma chamber.

Water, heated to near steam, moves through cracks in the rocks. Over time, the water leeches minerals out of the rock. These minerals are concentrated in solution in the water and are transported to other locations to precipitate as a vein.

The effect of migrating fluids tends to be localized, measured in 10's to 100's of yards. This type of metamorphism is usually associated with the presence of large plutons.

Index Minerals: select minerals used to measure the metamorphic grade, which reflects the intensity of the metamorphic process. The presence of a particular index mineral provides information about the temperature and pressure involved in a metamorphic event. Example: Garnet is classified as a mid-grade metamorphic rock.

As a general rule of thumb: the closer to the heat source, the greater the metamorphic effect.

Sedimentary Rocks

Sediments are basically various sized fragments of broken or eroded rock material. As weathering processes break down the parent material, the sediments are transported, sorted and deposited in piles. These sediment piles may lithify into sedimentary rocks.

Fragmentation, Transportation and Sorting

Wind and Running Water:

Wind is very effective in transporting sediments in areas of little vegetation. Example: The haze over the Grand Canyon is actually sand from Monument Valley, 50 miles away. Sand dunes are essentially piles of wind-blown micro-rock.

Pebbles in mountain pools and streambeds are pieces of the mountain broken off and carried to another location by water movement. The pebbles are polished and rounded by the abrasive action of tumbling into each other as the water carries them downstream.

The piles of sorted and transported sediment can be quite extensive in terms of depth and area covered. Example: Everything east of Richmond, Virginia is a sedimentary base. The sediments come from the erosion of the Appalachian Mountains.

The **velocity** achieved by most transport agents determines what and how far materials are transported, and those materials tend to be of relatively uniform size. The exception is those materials moved by glaciers.

A **glacier** acts like a giant bulldozer, moving most everything in its path, big or small.

Sizing (Fining)

Fining: the process of sorting materials by size.

Geologists describe sedimentary rocks by size. To determine the size, they use the **Wentworth Scale.**

Wentworth Scale

Name	Size	Analogy
Boulder	Larger than 256mm	Basketball
Cobbles	> 64mm and < 64mm	Tennis ball
Pebbles	> 2mm and < 64mm	Pea sized
Sand	1/16mm to 2mm	Coarse/ med/ fine grains
Silt	1/256mm to 1/16mm	none
Clay	Less than 1/256mm	none

There may be a variety of various sized sediments present in any given area. This size diversity represents that over time, a variety of transportation agents laid down the sedimentary material.

For the smaller sized materials, geologists can measure the size by passing the material through screens with different sized openings.

The point of determining size is to be able to recreate past environments. Size can provide clues to the original location of the material. Sedimentation is a continuous process.

Murky water: water carrying silt and clay sediments (suspended load) from upstream. Further upstream the materials are coarser.

The flowing water carries the material to the ocean where one of two things happen:

1. The material is deposited on the offshore continental shelf, or
2. The material is carried back inland to the inlets and bays.

Over time, the sediment thickly accumulates and may form typical coastal features such as sand bars and deltas. The continuous accumulation of sediment is why there is a continuing need to dredge harbors and rivers.

Lithification Processes:

The lithification processes of cementation, compaction/dessification, and precipitation form sedimentary rocks.

Cementation: Sedimentary materials deposited in a pile are of different sizes and, consequently, they have different sized spaces between grains. Some of these spaces are large enough to permit water flow through them. Sand-sized particles (or larger) have large spaces between them.

Groundwater has many chemicals in it. As water moves through the spaces, the pH – measure of acidity – changes, and drop by drop; chemicals are **precipitated** (deposited) along the edges of the grains. The spaces eventually become filled, and the precipitated chemicals hold the materials together.

The two most common cementing agents are silica and calcium carbonate.

Silica (SiO$_4$): Very hard (7 on the Mohs scale), the silica forms a rock that is difficult to break.

Calcium carbonate (CaCO$_3$): Less resistant to weathering, calcium carbonate is easily dissolved. Example: Navajo sandstone formations in the Zion National Park.

Chemical impurities in flowing groundwater may collect within the spaces between sediment grains. These impurities **cement** the grains together to form a rock.

Compaction and dessification: the processes that affect fine grain sediments.

Silt, clay and extremely fine sand get compressed by the weight (pressure) of the dirt and other materials on top of them and eventually dry out and lithify.

Precipitation: When chemicals in the groundwater precipitate as solutions in the underground cracks and crevices. Precipitation can be seen as chemicals deposited by the groundwater that have dried out on the surface of the material. Example: Water spots that harden on the shower walls.

The two most common precipitatory agents are silica and calcium carbonate.

Calcium carbonate formations are often found in caves, in the form of **stalactites** and **stalagmites.**

Stalactites form from the roof.
Stalagmites form on the floor. (Memory jogger: the "g" means ground up!)

The **geode** is an example of silica precipitation. Quartz crystals form inside a rock exterior. Precipitation doesn't occur between sediment grains, instead, whole cavities in existing rock material are filled.

Skill 2.4   Identify processes and products within the rock cycle.

The Rock Cycle

The **rock cycle** is a model that describes the various complex geologic processes that create, destroy, and modify rocks. The rock cycle model represents the ways in which rocks are continually modified, changing between igneous, sedimentary, and metamorphic, as they move through the cycle. For example, igneous rocks are those created by magma. Igneous rocks exposed at the surface may be broken down by erosion. The resultant sediments may later become lithified, turning into sedimentary rocks. Igneous or sedimentary rocks that are exposed to extreme heat and pressure beneath Earth's crust undergo changes without melting—these are metamorphic rocks. Any type of rock that is melted after it plunges beneath the surface turns back into igneous rock. As the rock cycle illustrates, any type of rock can be changed into any other type, if the conditions are right. In this sense, no rocks are truly created or destroyed, since they are all constantly being recycled.

The Rock Cycle

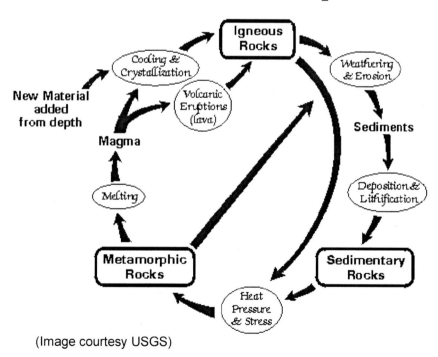

(Image courtesy USGS)

COMPETENCY 3.0 **KNOWLEDGE OF PLATE TECTONICS AND RELATED PROCESSES**

Skill 3.1 **Identify the historical development and supporting evidence that has led to the theory of plate tectonics.**

Plate Tectonics

Plate tectonic theory: Earth's surface is composed of lithospheric plates that "float" atop the asthenosphere and are in constant motion.

Plate tectonics: the study of the movement of the lithospheric plates and the consequences of that movement.

History of Tectonic Theory

At the beginning of the 20th century, most scientists accepted the view that Earth's materials were largely fixed in their positions, because rock was thought to be too hard and brittle to permit much movement.

Alfred Wegener & Continental Drift

In 1906, Alfred Wegener became intrigued by how the shape of the continents indicated that they at one time fit together. Wegener became convinced that the landmasses had—at one point in history—been connected, forming a giant supercontinent that he later dubbed Pangea. Most of his data and evidence is still included in the proofs offered for modern tectonic theory. Not surprisingly, his controversial theory of moveable continents was not readily accepted. Modern geology owes much to Alfred Wegener's initial postulations. The advent of new technologies has made it possible for science to verify most of his observations, and additional, new data has expanded Wegener's original concept into the widely accepted, modern theory of tectonics.

Evidence for Tectonic Theory

Shape of the continents: When graphically displayed, the continents look like they should largely fit together in a "jigsaw" puzzle fashion.

Paleomagnetism: As igneous rock cools, iron minerals within the rock will align much like a compass, to the magnetic pole. Scientific research has shown that the magnetic pole periodically—hundreds of thousands of years—reverses polarity.

Age of the rock: Besides being mirror images magnetically, dating research conducted on rocks on either side of a spreading center also indicate a mirroring of age. The age of the rock on either side of a spreading center are mirror images and get progressively older as you move away from the center. The youngest rock is always found directly at the spreading center. In comparison to continental rock materials, the youngest rock is found on the ocean floor, consistent with the tectonic theory of cyclic spreading and subduction.

Climatology: Cold areas show evidence of once having been hot and vice versa. For example, coal needs a hot and humid climate to form. It does not form in the areas of extreme cold. Although Antarctica is extremely cold, it has huge coal deposits. This indicates that at one time in the past, Antarctica must have been physically much closer to the equator.

Evidence of identical rock units: Rock units can be traced across ocean basins. Many rocks are distinctive in feature, composition, etc. Identical rock units have been found on multiple continents, usually along the edges of where the plates once apparently joined.

Topographic evidence: Topographic features can be traced across ocean basins. Some glacial deposits, stream channels, and mountain ranges terminate on one continent near the water's edge, and resume on another continent in relatively the same position.

Fossil evidence: Limited range fossils that could not swim or fly are found on either side of an ocean basin.

Sea turtle migration: The genetic instincts of sea turtles drive them to return to the islands where they hatched in order to lay eggs. The migration of the sea turtles over thousands of miles is well documented. The diverse location and number of islands to which the sea turtles migrate suggests that the plate movement has changed the location of the islands from their original position, immediately off shore of major continental masses.

Skill 3.2   Analyze the geologic processes involved in the movement of tectonic plates and the landforms produced by their movements.

Plate tectonic movement results from the motion induced in the lithosphere by convection the asthenosphere.

Plate boundaries are the points at which the edges of the tectonic plates abut.

There are three types of plate boundaries: divergent, convergent, and transform.

Divergent Boundaries

At a **divergent boundary**, or spreading center, two or more plates are moving away from one another. These boundaries generally occur in oceanic crust, and mark the location where new crust is created. As the plates pull apart, magma from the mantle rises up to fill the gap. As the magma cools and hardens, it forms a ridge along the spreading center. Such ridges make up the massive **mid-ocean ridge system** that exists throughout the world's ocean basins.

In some areas, divergent boundaries are forming on land. The initial stage of this formation is known as **rifting**, and an example can be found in Africa's Rift Valley. Here, the continent of Africa is being slowly split apart. Eventually, the rift will get deep and wide enough that a new ocean basin will be created, and a portion of what is now the African continent will form a new tectonic plate.

Convergent Boundaries

At a **convergent boundary**, the plates are moving toward and colliding with each other. These can occur in several geographic settings.

Ocean-ocean boundaries: Where two oceanic plates collide, one plate will slide beneath the other in a process called **subduction**. Generally, the older the oceanic crust is, the denser it is. Therefore, in an oceanic subduction zone the older plate slides beneath the younger one, forming a deep trench along the subduction zone. As the plate descends, it begins to melt, and the resultant magma rises to the surface forming a volcanic island chain. Eventually this chain will grow to be higher than sea level. Japan is an example of a volcanic island arc formed at an oceanic subduction zone.

Ocean-continental boundaries: Where an oceanic plate collides with a continental plate, the oceanic plate is subducted beneath the continental plate (because of its higher density). This process forms a deep trench, as well as melting of the descending oceanic plate. Magma from the melting plate rises up forming a volcanic mountain chain on land. The Andes Mountains in South America provide an example of a continental volcanic arc.

Continental-continental boundaries: In the case of two continental plates colliding, neither is dense enough to sink beneath the other. Instead, tremendous pressure causes the crust to buckle, forming huge mountains. The massive Himalayas are the result of a continental collision between the Indian and Eurasian plates.

Transform Boundaries

At a **transform boundary**, plates slide horizontally past one another. The majority of transform boundaries are found along the mid-ocean ridge system, where ridge segments are offset. In these areas, portions of the plates grind past one another laterally between the offset segments. Transform boundaries also occur on land. The San Andreas fault is possibly the most famous example of a transform boundary. Here, the Pacific Plate is moving horizontally past the North American plate, resulting in earthquake activity and mild deformation of the land surface.

Skill 3.3   Differentiate between the physical and chemical characteristics of oceanic crust and continental crust.

Oceanic crust and continental crust have different physical and chemical compositions. Oceanic crust is denser and thinner than continental crust. It is mainly composed of mafic rocks like basalt and gabbro. Continental crust is thicker and less dense, and is composed mainly of felsic rocks like granite.

Skill 3.4   Identify the types, causes, and effects of volcanoes.

Volcanic activity occurs wherever magma reaches the surface of Earth. This typically occurs at or near plate boundaries undergoing subduction or spreading, but may also occur away from the edges of plates, as a result of "hot spots."

Types of Volcanoes

Shield volcano: This type of volcano forms when the magma is silica-poor. Although the magma flows easily, it is still thick enough to pile up in layers and form the volcanic cone. The succeeding layers eventually build upward to form a massive volcanic mountain. The cone is tall (up to 9,000 meters), broad across, and composed of overlapping layers of lava flow. The lava cools quickly and resembles asphalt in appearance. Because shield volcanoes are produced over hot spots and at spreading centers, the broadest and tallest parts are usually underwater. The eruptions are characteristically very quiet with lots of lava and little ash. The lava travels slowly unless moving downhill. These eruptions are generally non-lethal because there is plenty of time to get out of the way of the slow moving lava. The eruptions occur over a long period of time (years).

Composite volcano: These volcanoes, also known as stratovolcanoes, form from lava eruptions coupled with pyroclastic explosions. They are composed of layers of lava alternating with layers of pyroclastic deposits. They tend to have a steep summit (with a summit crater) and are more gently sloping lower down. Composite volcanoes have thick, viscous lavas that do not travel great distances. They tendt o be explosive and eject huge quantities of pyroclastic material. Composite volcanoes are common along the "Ring of Fire," where active subduction is occurring. Their explosivity makes them extremely dangerous volcanoes.

Cinder cone volcano: This type of volcano forms from thick, silica rich magma that does not easily flow. However, it is the local concentrations of gas in the magma that cause the eruptions that build cinder cones, not the silica content. Cinder cones have steep sides, and are built up from ash and cinders ejected from a central vent. They are the most common type of volcano, and are often formed in one eruptive event. They often form on the flanks of shield volcanoes.

Effects of volcanoes include **nuée ardentes** (glowing, highly heated masses of gas-charged lava that race down the slopes of a volcano), volcanic mudflows (called **lahars**), lava flows, flooding, fires, and the ejection of particulate and other pyroclastic materials into the air.

Classification of Volcanoes

Volcanoes are classified by their activity:
- Active volcano: a volcano that is actively erupting, producing steam, ash, and lava.
- Dormant volcano: a volcano that is not presently erupting, but the geologic conditions exist for future eruptions.
- Extinct volcano: a volcano that is not presently erupting and the geologic conditions do not favor any further eruptions.

Skill 3.5   Identify the causes and effects of earthquakes.

Earthquakes occur when Earth materials in the lithosphere rupture. The sudden breaking of the rock material causes a release of energy. As tectonic plates try to move past one another, rock near the plate boundary stretches, causing it to store elastic energy. When the elastic energy overcomes the frictional forces that are resisting the movement of the rock, the rock materials suddenly move along the rupture, or **fault**. This causes motion in the rock that creates vibrations which travel through Earth. These vibrations are felt as an earthquake. The point deep underground where the rock breaks is called the **focus**. The point on the surface directly above the focus is called the **epicenter**. The energy released during an earthquake travels outward in the form of seismic waves.

Effects of Earthquakes

Shaking: The extent of the shaking is dependent on the type of material the seismic wave encounters. Soft material amplifies the shaking.

Ground displacement: The ground literally drops away. Vertical displacements of over 20 feet occurred during the 1964 earthquake in Anchorage, Alaska.

Ground cracks: Cracks can open either several inches or several feet.

Structural damage: The shaking during an earthquake often breaks the man-made structures in the area. The structures collapse, killing, injuring, or trapping the people inside.

Landslides: Loose material is set into motion by Earthquake.

Fires: Gas and electric lines break during earthquakes, sparking and feeding fires. Water mains are also often broken, limiting the means to fight the fires.

Liquefaction: In an earthquake, sand and silt liquefy, developing the consistency of "quicksand." Packed sand and silt have trace amounts of water between the grains. As the shaking occurs, these move apart and more water enters. If there is a low water table, the grains eventually become flooded with water in the spaces. As the material liquefies, the structures built upon them sink. However, the material does not have the same rate of liquefaction, and only parts of the buildings sink, causing their structural collapse.

Tsunamis: Earthquakes can trigger underwater landslides or cause sea floor displacements that in turn generate deep waves in all directions. Far out to sea these waves may be hardly noticeable. However, as they near the shoreline, the shallowing of the sea floor forces the waves upward in a "springing" motion. The tidal waves formed by the upward motion can grow to be quite immense and powerful depending on the topography of the sea floor and the magnitude of earthquake.

Skill 3.6   Distinguish between the characteristics of seismic waves.

Seismic waves are energy waves that are generated when rocks fracture during an earthquake. Seismic waves travel out from their source in all directions. There are two main types of seismic waves: body waves and surface waves. Body waves can travel right through Earth, while surface waves move along the surface.

P waves and **S waves** are both types of body waves. P waves move the fastest, and arrive at seismic recording stations first. P waves can move through both solids and liquids, and therefore are able to travel directly through Earth. P waves are also called compressional waves because they push and pull in the direction they are moving. S waves are slower than P waves, and cannot travel through liquids. Therefore, they cannot travel through Earth's liquid outer core. The movement in an S wave is up and down, perpendicular to the wave's direction of travel.

Love waves and **Rayleigh waves** are two types of surface waves. They travel through Earth's crust. Love waves are the fastest surface waves, and their motion is side to side. Rayleigh waves roll along the surface just like ocean waves roll across the water. Most of the shaking from an earthquake is caused by Rayleigh waves.

Skill 3.7   Identify how the movement of tectonic plates has influenced climate (e.g. hydrosphere, geosphere, biosphere).

There are several ways in which the movement of tectonic plates affects climate. The distribution and movement of tectonic plates affects oceanic and atmospheric circulation, which in turn affects the planet's heat distribution and weather patterns. Plate motion is responsible for the creation of mountain ranges, which have their own affect on climate. Also, plate tectonics is the driving force behind volcanic eruptions. When volcanoes erupt, carbon dioxide—a greenhouse gas—is released into the atmosphere.

The **distribution of landmasses** has changed through time with the movement of tectonic plates. The distribution of Earth's landmasses affects climates in a few ways:

- Land areas at high latitudes experience greater snow and ice accumulation since less incoming solar radiation reaches high latitudes as compared to low latitudes. Therefore, if landmasses are concentrated at high latitudes, there will be significant accumulation of snow and ice.
- There are differences in albedo (the amount of energy reflected by a surface) between land and water. The ratio of land to water, especially in the lower latitudes, therefore has an effect on the amount of solar energy reflected or absorbed.
- The paths of ocean currents—which distribute heat globally—are governed by the positions of the continents; as these positions change, so do the paths of ocean currents.

The **elevation of landmasses** also plays a significant role in the determination of climate. Higher areas are colder. Cold areas may experience year round snow and ice, which in turn increases albedo. Furthermore, mountains have an affect on local climate. The windward sides tend to be wet, while the leeward sides are generally dry. Regions of elevated terrain also affect atmospheric circulation patterns.

Plate tectonics also affects global **volcanic activity**. Faster rates of plate motion correlate with increased volcanic activity. Because volcanoes release carbon dioxide into the atmosphere, which in turn traps more heat in the atmosphere, increased volcanism can lead to a global increase in temperature.

COMPETENCY 4.0 KNOWLEDGE OF EARTH'S SURFACE PROCESSES

Skill 4.1   **Compare physical and chemical weathering and their effects on landforms.**

Weathering: the physical and chemical breakdown and alteration of rocks and minerals at or near Earth's surface.

Mechanical (or physical) weathering occurs when rock is broken into smaller pieces with no change in chemical or mineralogical composition. The resulting material still resembles the original material. Example: Rock pieces breaking off of a boulder. The pieces still resemble the original material, but on a smaller scale.

Chemical weathering occurs where a chemical or mineralogical change occurs in the rock and the resulting material no longer resembles the original material. Example: Granite eventually weathers into sand, silt, and clay particles.

Weathering is typically caused by a combination of chemical and mechanical processes.

Types of Mechanical Weathering

Frost wedging: This occurs when rock has a crack in it. Water collects in the crack and then freezes. Over time, as this cycle repeats itself, the expanding water gradually pushes the rock apart.

Salt crystal growth: In a process similar to frost wedging, as the water evaporates, it leaves salt crystals behind. Eventually, these crystals build up and push the rock apart. This is a very small-scale effect and takes considerably longer than frost wedging to affect the rock material.

Abrasion: This is a key factor in mechanical weathering. The motion of landscape materials produces significant weathering effects, scouring, chipping, or wearing away pieces of material. Abrasive agents include wind blown sand, water movement, and the movement of materials in landslides.

Biological Activity: This is a two-fold weathering agent.

> **Plants:** Seeds will sometimes land and begin to grow in a crack in a rock. The root structure eventually acts as a wedge, pushing the rock apart.

> **Animals:** As animals burrow, the displaced material has an abrasive effect on the surrounding rock. Because of the limited number of burrowing animals, plant activity has a much greater weathering effect.

Pressure release (exfoliation): Rock expands when compressive forces are removed, and bits of the rock break off during expansion. This can result in massive rock formations with rounded edges. Example: Half-Dome in Yosemite National Park.

Thermal expansion and contraction: Minerals within a rock will expand or contract due to changes in temperature. Dependent on the minerals in the rock, this expansion and contraction occurs at different rates and magnitudes. Essentially, the rock internally tears itself apart. The rock may look solid but when placed under pressure, easily crumbles.

Climate is a key factor in mechanical weathering.

Types of Chemical Weathering

Oxidation (rust): Oxygen atoms become incorporated into the formula of a mineral in a rock and the mineral becomes unstable and breaks off in flakes. Example: Iron oxide (FeO_2) changes to iron trioxide (FeO_3) due to the oxygen chemically imparted to the mineral.

Solution: Due to their inherent composition, some minerals found in rocks easily dissolve into solution when exposed to a liquid. Example: Halite (rock salt) completely dissolves in water.

Acids: Water and water vapor may combine with other elements and gases to form acids. Water (H_2O) and carbon dioxide (CO_2) can chemically combine to become carbonic acid (H_2CO_3). Sulfur dioxide (SO_2) particles can chemically combine with water (H_2O) to form sulfuric acid (H_2SO_4). Generally found in combination with solution, acids cause the majority of chemical weathering.

Biological Activity: Plant roots growing in the cracks of rocks not only cause mechanical wedging, but also secrete acids that cause chemical weathering.

Common Effects of Weathering

Quartz: Inert to most effects, quartz stays in the environment as original material.

Feldspar: forms clay minerals.

Ferromags: Also form clay minerals. Example: Gneiss/schist can erode to clay minerals as the quartz is leeched out, and blown or transported away.

Carbonates: Highly susceptible to carbonic acids, carbonates and carbonated rocks such as limestone will–dependent on the concentration of acid–dissolve into solution and/or become riddled with holes.

Differential Weathering

Differential weathering occurs when rocks on a landscape weather at different rates. The effect of this difference can create fantastic landscape features, with some rocks "sticking up," arched, or nested in deep depressions. Examples: Ship Rock, Devil's Tower, and the other mesa and butte formations in Monument Valley.

Skill 4.2   Analyze the principles and processes of sedimentation (i.e., erosion, deposition).

See Skill 2.3, section on sedimentary rocks.

Skill 4.3   Identify the properties of aquifers and the movement of groundwater through sediments and rock formations.

Both groundwater and surface water resources are derived from rainfall, though over very different timeframes. After it falls, rain may evaporate, infiltrate into soils, or run off into streams, rivers, or saltwater areas. If it evaporates or runs off into saltwater areas, it is unavailable to humans for use (for most purposes). Drinking water, agriculture, livestock water, and most industrial uses all require freshwater, which may come from groundwater or surface water.

If rainfall infiltrates into subsurface rock, whether or not it forms groundwater depends on whether enough water is present to fully saturate the area. A permeable rock body that is able to transmit water to wells and springs is known as an **aquifer**, and the level that the groundwater will rise to within the soil is known as the **water table**. The various types of aquifers are shown in the figure on the next page.

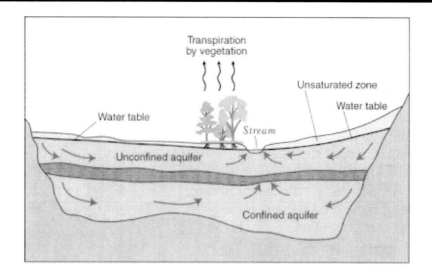

EXPLANATION

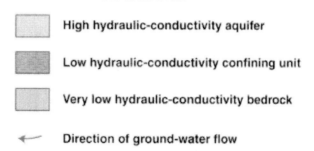

High hydraulic-conductivity aquifer

Low hydraulic-conductivity confining unit

Very low hydraulic-conductivity bedrock

Direction of ground-water flow

Unconfined aquifers are generally closer to the surface and have no confining or low-permeability layers between the groundwater and the surface. Unconfined aquifers can be easily replenished by rainfall and can also be easily accessed by shallow wells. Unconfined aquifers are more susceptible to pollution because they are closer to the surface and vulnerable to contaminants that are introduced into the soil or surface water. Unconfined groundwater may replenish streams or lakes if the bottom of the stream or lake is below the water table. Conversely, streams or lakes may replenish surface aquifers during periods of high rainfall and runoff. Unconfined aquifers can be considered renewable resources if they can be replenished as quickly as they are used. If depleted, they can often be replenished by cutting back on groundwater extraction for a time.

Confined aquifers are generally deeper and separated from the ground surface by a layer of impermeable or low-permeability material—often a clay or silt layer within the soil. Confined aquifers were originally also derived from rainfall, but may be millennia old. These aquifers are not as easily replenished once the groundwater is removed, because there is no easy way for rainfall to reach them. Often these deposits of groundwater were formed long ago and are now in relatively arid areas. Deep wells may be drilled to access them as water resources, but they are not necessarily renewable resources. If too much groundwater is removed from confined aquifers, the ground surface may subside.

When rainfall runs off, it produces **surface water resources** in the form of streams, rivers, and lakes. These resources may be produced by rainfall or by snowmelt in the spring and summer. Surface water resources are renewable but ephemeral and dependent on the weather each year. If there is less rainfall or snowfall than normal, or if patterns of precipitation are unusual, communities that depend on these resources may need to conserve water that year or use a backup source. Most drinking water taken from surface water resources is removed from rivers near the headwaters to reduce the potential for contamination and the need for treatment. Like groundwater, competition for surface water resources is increasing among groups who wish to use it for drinking water, agriculture and livestock, hydropower, and conservation of water flow for habitat and protection of aquatic life.

In sediments or soils, **porosity** refers to the amount of void or open space between grains. It is usually represented as a percentage or fraction from 0-1. In very loose sediments with large, round grains, porosity can be as high as 50%. In poorly-sorted sediments with a variety of grain sizes, smaller particles fill the voids and porosity can range down to 20-30%. Rocks have much lower porosity, with sedimentary rocks being more porous than granitic rocks, which may have a porosity as low as 0.01 (1%). Fractures in the rock may also increase porosity and affect water flow in unpredictable ways. This is known as **secondary porosity**.

Permeability is the ability of sediments or soils to allow the flow of water or another liquid such as oil. Permeability is related to porosity, but also depends on the size and connectedness of the pore spaces. Permeability is expressed in units of cm^2. Generally, sandy or gravelly soils are much more permeable than clays or silts, even though clays and silts have a relatively high porosity. In clays and silts the pore spaces are so small that it is hard for water to pass through them. Water has a high **surface tension**, and therefore it cannot penetrate into very small spaces.

Permeability values of 10^{-3} to 10^{-6} cm^2 are considered to be high-medium permeability and make good groundwater aquifers (often sands and gravel or highly fractured rock), while permeability values of 10^{-11} cm^2 or smaller (often silts and clays or unfractured rock) are considered impermeable and are barriers to flow. Permeability is measured in the laboratory or the field using a pump test.

Water pressure is the height at which water will rise in a well, also known as **hydraulic head**. The height of water in an unconfined aquifer is known as the **water table**, which may fluctuate with rainfall, tides, or human extraction. Aquifers confined by a low-permeability layer may contain water under higher pressure. If a well is drilled into such an aquifer, the water may rise higher than the confining layer.

These various properties are combined into **Darcy's Law**, which predicts the rate of discharge of water through soils or sediment:

$$Q = \frac{-\kappa A}{\mu} \frac{(P_b - P_a)}{L}$$

where:
Q = discharge volume of water (cm^3/sec)
κ = intrinsic permeability of soil or sediment (cm^2)
A = cross-sectional area through which the water flows (cm^2)
P_b - P_a = water pressure change over the distance L (Pa)
μ = viscosity of water (Pa-sec)
L = distance (cm)

This equation is also frequently written as:

$$q = -K(\Delta h / \Delta l)$$

where:
q = Darcy flow velocity (cm/sec)
K = hydraulic conductivity (cm/sec)
Δh = change in water pressure or hydraulic head (m)
Δl = distance over which water travels (m)

The quantity ($\Delta h / \Delta l$), also notated as i, is known as the **hydraulic gradient**, or the change in hydraulic head over distance. Notice that water only flows from higher to lower hydraulic head, which is why the sign of the equation is negative. The greater the hydraulic gradient, the greater the flow will be.

The Darcy flow velocity q assumes that water takes a straight path through the aquifer. However, water actually has to navigate through the pore spaces and because of this, takes an indirect path through the sediments. The actual velocity of the water required to navigate through the pore spaces and create the Darcy flow is called the **mean porewater velocity**, and is higher than the Darcy velocity. This quantity is given by the following equation:

$$v = q/\phi$$

where:
v = mean porewater velocity (cm/sec)
q = Darcy flow velocity
ϕ = porosity

Example: What is the mean porewater velocity in a sandy aquifer with a hydraulic conductivity of 1.5 cm/sec and a porosity of 0.43, if the hydraulic head decreases by 10 m over a distance of 1 km?

Solution:
First, use the flow version of Darcy's law to calculate the Darcy flow velocity:
q = -1.5 cm/sec x -10 m / 1000 m = 0.015 cm/sec

Next, use the equation for mean porewater velocity to find the solution:

v = 0.015 cm/sec / 0.43 = 0.035 cm/sec

Skill 4.4   Analyze the movement of water through the hydrologic cycle, including energy changes that occur as water changes phase.

The **hydrologic cycle** is driven by solar radiation. The cycle of evaporation from the oceans, and precipitation over land is the methodology employed by nature to maintain the water balance at any given location. Earth constantly recycles water. It evaporates from the sea, falls as rain, and flows over the land as it returns to the ocean. Reservoirs for water on Earth include rivers, lakes, ponds, the oceans, ice caps, snowfields, glaciers, groundwater, and the atmosphere. The constant circulation of water among these reservoirs comprises the hydrologic cycle.

Evaporation

In a closed system, a rise in temperature is accompanied by a rise in pressure. However, in the case of the hydrologic cycle where the system is relatively open, a rise in temperature is not necessarily accompanied by a rise in pressure. The increase in temperature in comparison to the surroundings causes high-speed molecules within the water to attempt to change phase (to become a gas).

In a closed system phase equilibrium is reached where the flow of molecules caused by the rise in temperature and ambient pressure is roughly equal, and if the temperature rises further, more high-speed molecules escape into a gaseous state and the liquid boils away. However, in an open system such as the oceans, the release of molecules from liquid into a gaseous state continues without reaching equilibrium. As the molecules are continually removed, the liquid to gas process (evaporation) continues until no liquid is left.

Given the volume of the oceans and the relatively cool temperatures involved, the oceans simply evaporate a thin layer of water, rather than the entire ocean. So why don't the oceans boil? Several factors keep this from happening. First, the temperature of the water is generally well below that required to boil water and the salinity of the water further raises the boiling point. Also, the remaining molecules (the slower ones), absorb heat from their surroundings (endothermic), and in effect, help cause the ocean to remain relatively cool. Additionally, the atmospheric pressure remains constant, keeping the amount of high-speed molecules at a minimum.

Condensation/Precipitation

Precipitation is generally just the reverse process. As the heated, energetic water molecules in gaseous form rise in altitude, they encounter a different pressure and temperature environment and cool, giving off heat (exothermic). Eventually they cool enough to condense—return to a liquid phase—and fall back to the surface, usually in the form of rain.

Runoff

Runoff refers to the process of water traveling over the surface to a river, lake, ocean, etc. Runoff carries water from rainfall and snowmelt along the surface to a larger body of water, where it rejoins the cycle of evaporation and precipitation again.

Transpiration

When plants lose water from their leaves directly into the air, this process is known as transpiration. Like evaporation, this process also adds water vapor back to the atmosphere.

Energy Transfers

Matter can change state if enough heat (energy) is applied or removed. As water moves through various stage of the hydrologic cycle, it changes state (phase) and has an accompanying energy transfer. This transfer is based upon the basic laws of physics and chemistry in that it will involve either an exothermic or endothermic reaction.

As the cycle begins over the oceans, the solar radiation heats the water sufficiently to cause the liquid to change phase.

Water and the States of Energy

Specific Heat: the amount of heat required to raise or lower the temperature of one gram of a substance by one degree Celsius.

Heat Capacity: the ability of a substance to resist a change in temperature. Water has an extremely high heat capacity. It is very resistant to a change in temperature. It takes a great deal of energy transfer to heat up water, but it also takes a great amount of energy loss to cool it down. When we heat water we are actually transferring energy from a heat source to the water. The water molecules absorb the energy and move faster. This causes the temperature of the water to rise.

Latent Heat: the amount of heat required to change matter from one state to another. Example: The amount of heat required to cause evaporation or condensation of water.

Heat of Vaporization: the amount of heat energy required to change 1 gram of water from a liquid to a vapor, or back. The heat of vaporization is equal to 540 cal/gram. Example: 1 gram of water at 99 degrees C requires 1 calorie of heat to raise the temperature to 100°C, which is the boiling point of water. However, the water will not turn into steam (vapor or gas), until an additional 540 calories are added because of the high heat capacity of water. The requirement for additional calories to force a change of state works in our favor. Without the law of heat of vaporization, the oceans would rapidly vaporize!

Rain represents the opposite pattern. In rain, 540 calories have been removed, changing the state of water from a vapor (gas) to a liquid.

Heat of fusion: the amount of heat energy expressed in calories required to change 1 gram of water from a solid to a liquid, or back. The heat of fusion is equal to 80 cal/gram.

There is a difference in the amount of heat required to change states between liquids, solids, and vapors.

It takes more heat to change from a liquid to a vapor, or a vapor to a liquid, than it does to change from a solid to a liquid, or a liquid to a solid.

Water is a dynamic factor in our atmosphere because its resistance to change state allows Earth to maintain a temperature balance in the presence and absence of solar radiation (i.e. day and night).

Skill 4.5   Evaluate the origin and distribution of freshwater resources in Florida.

The majority of Florida's freshwater supply exists as groundwater, which is replenished by rainfall. Freshwater in Florida also exists in rivers, lakes, springs, and wetlands.

Most of Florida's groundwater comes from the Floridian Aquifer, which provides the municipal water supply for several cities. It is one of the most productive aquifers in the world. The Biscayne Aquifer, located in the southeastern part of the state, is another important aquifer. Additionally, there are three other principal aquifers that provide drinking water for various areas of the state.
Florida's major streams include the Apalachicola River, the Suwannee River, the Choctawhatchee River, the Escambia River, the St. John's River, the Kissimmee River, the Peace River, the Withlacoochee River, and the Hillsborough River. These streams are located in the north and central part of the state, while drainage patterns in southern Florida are more poorly developed.

Florida has thousands of lakes, the largest of which is Lake Okeechobee. Located in central southern Florida, the lake covers about 700 square miles. The lake was formed roughly 6,000 years ago when ocean waters receded and left the body of water now called Okeechobee standing in a shallow depression.

Florida's more than 700 springs comprise the largest concentration of freshwater springs on the planet. Most of Florida's springs originated from sinkhole activity. Limestone, which underlies virtually all of Florida, is readily dissolved by acidic rainwater. As cavities form in limestone bedrock, sinkholes form. Springs are created when the groundwater level is high enough that it intersects with the surface of the ground.

Florida also has many freshwater marshes and wetlands. The Florida Everglades is the largest marsh system in the U.S. Diversion of water and draining of the Everglades has drastically reduced the size of the marsh, which once covered over 3,000,000 acres.

Skill 4.6 Discriminate between landforms and sedimentary deposits created by water, wind, and ice

Sedimentary **landforms** are carved out of the land while **deposits** are placed there over time.

Water:

Running Water:

Erosional landforms created by rivers include:

Stream channels: Carved into sediment or bedrock by the flow of water. Channels in alluvial materials may be **meandering** (with sweeping bends) or **braided** (with a network of diverging and converging channels).

Oxbow lakes: Sometimes a meandering stream erodes its channel in a way that cuts off one of the meander bends, eventually leaving it abandoned. When a meander becomes completely cut off from the main flow of the river, it is called and oxbow lake.

Stream terraces: When a stream cuts down into its channel, it may leave behind its former floodplain. Where former floodplains exists in the form of flat surfaces, above the present stream channel, they are known as stream terraces.

V-shaped valleys: River valleys in mountainous landscapes have a distinct V-shape, in contrast with glacial valleys, which are U-shaped.

Depositional landforms created by rivers include:

Deltas: A delta forms where a stream enters a quieter body of water, such as an ocean or lake. The velocity of flow abruptly slows down, causing the river to deposit it sediment load in the form of a delta. The Mississippi Delta is an example of a large delta where the Mississippi River meets the Gulf of Mexico.

Alluvial fans: Alluvial fans are analogous to a delta on land. They result from the buildup of sediments deposited at the mouth of a valley where streams emerge from a mountainous area to a relatively lower, flatter area.

Floodplains: As a river periodically overflows its banks during floods, sediments are deposited along either side of the channel. Over time, these sediments build up a flat area known as a floodplain.

Natural levees: As a river overflows its banks during a flood, its velocity decreases, causing it to deposit its suspended sediment. The coarsest sediment is deposited first, along the channel edges. Over time this sediment builds up a natural levee along the border of the channel.

Groundwater:

Erosional landforms created by groundwater include:

Karst topography: Karst topography occurs in areas underlain by carbonate bedrock, such as limestone. Groundwater is very effective in dissolving limestone, forming caves and sinkholes. Chemical leaching combined with groundwater produces Carbonic acid ($CO_2 + H_2O = H_2CO_3$), and this acid dissolves the limestone, riddling an area with underground holes.

Karst Features:

Cave: A cave is an empty space beneath the ground surface. The majority of caves are formed by carbonate dissolution.

Sinkhole: Often a void, such as a cave, will fill with water. During times of drought, the water may recede from the cave. When this happens, the unsupported weight of the cave ceiling may collapse, forming a sinkhole. Sinkholes are unpredictable in terms of when and where they will occur. They can be huge in scope, swallowing up entire city blocks, and can become small lakes dotting the landscape.

Depositional landforms created by groundwater include:

Speleotherm: Speleothem is a general term for a deposit in a cave. The majority of these forms are either stalactites or stalagmites.

Stalactite: Cave deposits that hang from the ceiling are called stalactites.

Stalagmite: Cave deposits built up from the floor of a cave are called stalagmites.

Column: Columns are mineral formations at the top and bottom of the cave that have joined together.

Wind

Erosional Landforms:

Deflation: Deflation refers to the lifting and removing of loose material and sediment.

Blowout: Deflation can cause a blowout—a wind eroded depression in the land surface.

Ventifact: Although wind seldom moves particles larger than sand grains, the wind-blown sand can act as a giant scouring agent, shaping isolated boulders, cobble, and pebbles into ventifacts which are rocks with flat, wind-eroded surfaces.

Yardang: A yardang is a large, wind-sculpted landform with an orientation parallel to the direction of the prevailing wind.

Desert pavement (regolith): As wind removes fine sediments from the ground surface, a thin, closely packed layer of gravel is left behind. This desert pavement helps to protect the surface from further deflation.

Depositional Landforms:

Loess deposits: Large deposits of wind-blown silt are known as loess deposits.

Sand dunes: Sand dunes are large ridges or mounds of sand deposited by wind.

Dune Forms:

The type of sand dune formed is dependent on the velocity and direction of the wind, the supply of sand available, and the presence and or distribution of vegetation.

Barchan dunes: Crescent-shaped sand dunes with crescent horns pointing downwind are called barchan dunes. These develop in areas with limited sand supply and are usually separated from one another as they move across the bare ground. The barchan dune is the most common type of sand dune.

Transverse dunes: Transverse dunes are nearly straight, elongated sand dunes, oriented perpendicular to the wind. These form in areas where the sand supply is abundant.

Parabolic dunes: Parabolic dunes are deeply curved sand dunes that commonly form around a blowout, especially near a beach. The horns of the curve point upwind and are usually anchored by vegetation.

Longitudinal dunes: Longitudinal dunes are large, symmetrical sand ridge formed parallel to the wind direction. This type of dune often forms the largest dune of all the types (200 meters high, 120 km in length).

Star dunes: Isolated hills of sand that have a complex form, star dunes are found mainly in parts of the Arabian and Sahara deserts. They are shaped like multi-pointed stars, and occur where the wind direction varies.

Wind ripples: small, low ridges of sand grains similar to those produced by sediment deposited by a current in water. Sand moves perpendicular to the ridges and indicates the direction of movement.

Coastal dunes: Where there is a large supply of beach sand and steady winds, coastal dunes may develop. These dunes are typically colonized by plants, which increases their stability.

Ice

Erosional Landforms:

Glacial striations: Long scratches and grooves in bedrock, called glacial striations, form when rocks embedded in the ice at the bottom of a glacier gouge the rock surface.

Glacial valleys: As a glacier erodes a mountain valley, the valley comes to take on a characteristic U-shape.

Truncated spurs: Triangular-shaped cliffs called truncated spurs result when a glacier erodes ridges of land that extended from the highland into the valley.

Hanging valleys: During glaciation, many small glaciers may form in tributary valleys that feed into the main valley glacier. When the glaciers recede, these valleys are left standing above the main valley, and are therefore known as hanging valleys.

Pater noster lakes: A series of water-filled depressions in the floor of a glacial valley, pater noster lakes result from the plucking and scouring of bedrock by glacial ice.

Cirques: A cirque is a bowl-shaped depression at the head of a glacial valley. They are characterized by steep walls on three sides, with an opening on the down-valley side.

Fjords: Steep-sided, deep inlets from the sea are called fjords. They form from glacial troughs that became drowned when sea levels rose following the ice age.

Arêtes and horns: Arêtes are sharp ridges and horns are sharp peaks, both formed by the action of glaciers plucking and enlarging cirques.

Roches moutonnées: Roches moutonnées are asymmetrical hills formed in protruding bedrock ridges by glaciers. An advancing glacier smooths a gently sloping surface facing the ice sheet, while it plucks a steep face on the opposite side of the ridge.

Depositional Landforms:

Material deposited directly by a glacier is known as **till**. Material deposited by glacial meltwater is referred to as **drift**.

Glacial erratics: Large boulders lying on the surface that have been transported far from their area of origin are known as glacial erratics.

Moraines: Moraines are landforms composed of glacial till. **Lateral moraines** are ridges of till lying parallel to the direction of a glaciers movement. **Medial moraines** form when two parallel alpine glaciers meet to form a single glacier. The lateral moraines from both glaciers form a single dark stripe of till down the center of the ice stream. **End moraines** form at the terminus of a glacier. An end moraine that marks the outer limit of a glacier's extent is also known as a **terminal moraine**. End moraines that were created during stable periods of a glacier's ongoing retreat are referred to as **recessional moraines**.

Drumlins: Drumlins are elongated, smooth, parallel hills formed largely out of till.

Outwash plains: The sediment deposited by meltwater ahead of a glacier forms an area called an outwash plain.

Kettles: Basins or depressions formed by isolated blocks of ice are known as kettles.

Kames: Kames are mounds of glacial drift deposited by meltwater.

Eskers: Narrow ridges of drift deposited by meltwater when a glacier is stagnant are called eskers.

Skill 4.7   Identify the geologic features of Florida and the processes that produced them

Karst terrain: Florida is underlain by carbonate rocks, which are susceptible to dissolution by water. This dissolution results in sinkholes, caves, springs, and underground streams, all of which are features of karst topography.

Coral reefs: Ancient coral reefs make up the islands of the Florida Keys. Seaward of the Keys, living reefs grow today.

Surface geology: As sea levels rose and fell throughout recent geologic history, Florida was repeatedly covered with sediments that washed over the land. Most of Florida's surface geology is comprised of carbonates, and fine-grained clastic sedimentary rocks.

COMPETENCY 5.0 KNOWLEDGE OF MAPPING AND REMOTE SENSING

Skill 5.1 **Identify surface features from topographic maps, photographs, and satellite images.**

A **topographic map** is a special kind of map intended to highlight natural features and the contours of the land. Topographic maps are frequently used by surveyors, engineers, and for outdoor activities such as hiking and hunting. See Skill 5.2 for an example of a topographic map.

Identifying features on a topographic map relies upon an understanding of **contour lines**. Contour lines connect points of equal elevation. If you were walking along a contour line you would be neither gaining nor losing elevation. The **contour interval** indicates the change in elevation that occurs between two adjacent contour lines. Here is a list of some common landforms explaining how they are represented on topographic maps:

Stream valleys: Stream valleys are represented by contour lines forming a V shape. The point of the V points in the upstream direction.

Hills: Hills are represented by contour lines in concentric circles.

Ridges: A ridge is represented by U-shaped or V-shaped contour lines, where the closed end of the line points *away* from high ground. (The opposite as with a stream valley.)

Depressions: Depressions are represented by close contour lines with tick marks pointing into the center.

Cliffs: Cliffs are represented by very closely spaced contour lines, possibly even touching one another.

Aerial photographs and **satellite images** can also be used to identify surface features. On the next page, a false-color satellite image of a portion of south Florida is shown. In this case, as with many aerial or satellite photos, no additional information is provided on the image to assist with interpretation. However, the boundary between water and land can still be interpreted, and manmade features are relatively visible. In general, irregular outlines will represent natural features, and square or circular features and straight lines will represent manmade features and built-up land. It is possible to identify some major roads in the image below. Keys and atolls can be clearly seen. Light pink and green areas represent developed land. In interpreting these images, reference to a map can sometimes be helpful. Locating a prominent feature on a satellite or aerial photograph (such as a mountain peak, major highway, river, etc.) can help you orient the image with a reference map and/or your surroundings if you are using the image for field work in a given area.

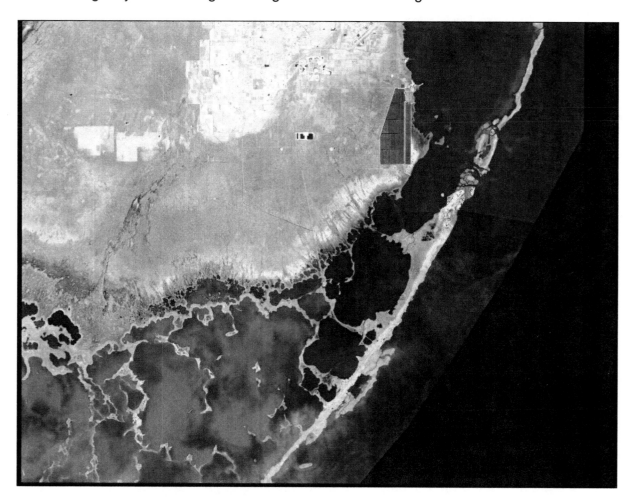

Skill 5.2   Interpret topographic and oceanographic maps.

A **topographic map** is a special kind of map intended to highlight natural features and the contours of the land. Topographic maps are frequently used by surveyors and engineers, and for outdoor activities such as hiking and hunting. A **bathymetric map** is a topographic map showing underwater features or coastlines, and is used for navigation and exploration for natural resources.

The topographic map below is of the area around Stowe, Vermont, and shows a variety of natural and man-made features. Green areas are vegetated areas, and rivers and lakes are shown in blue. Land elevation contours are shown using brown lines. These lines indicate lines of constant elevation.

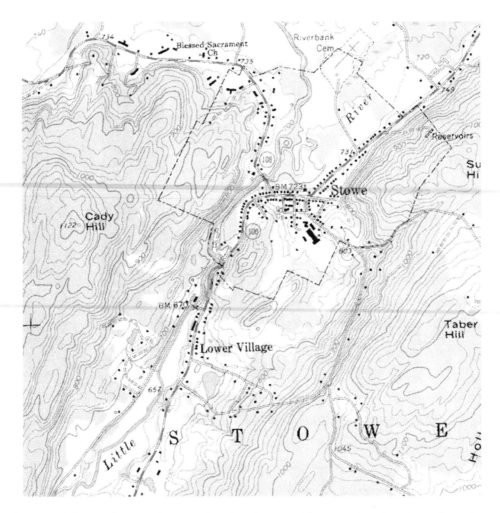

Concentric contours decreasing in size and increasing in elevation denote a hill or mountain, and the elevation of the peak is normally shown (such as for Cady Hill, above). Concentric contours decreasing in elevation and size denote a basin or depression. Sharp V-shaped contours frequently indicate a river valley. Closely spaced contours indicate a steeper slope, while widely spaced contours indicate a flatter area.

White areas show developed areas (or other areas barren of vegetation, such as rocky mountaintops), with individual buildings shown as black dots (larger scale maps may not show these details). Densely built-up areas may be shown in red or gray. Smaller paved roads are drawn as two parallel lines, and dashed parallel lines show small, unpaved roads. Trails (not indicated on this map) may be shown as single, continuous or dashed lines. Larger roads are indicated with red and white stripes, and are designated with highway numbers. City names and boundaries are shown, along with other municipal features, such as reservoirs and a graveyard.

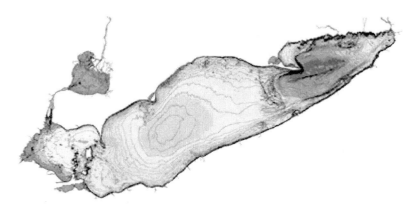

The bathymetric map above shows depth contours for Lake Erie and Lake St. Clair. In this case, the blue lines are contours of constant depth. Shallower areas are shaded in red and yellow, areas of medium depth are shown in green, and deeper areas are shown in light and dark blue. This map is an example of the use of color shading to make a topographic or bathymetric map easier to read and visualize. In coastal maps, shades of blue are typically used for water areas, with darker blue at deeper depths, and shades of green, yellow, and brown are used for decreasing depth of water or increasing land elevations.

Skill 5.3   Compare landforms illustrated on maps and imagery to geologic processes.

Landforms are large-scale natural features of Earth, which can be observed in photographs and on topographic maps. Continental landforms include features like valleys, mountains, hills, plateaus, plains, and ice.

Valleys are depressions between higher elevation areas such as mountains, hills, or plateaus. They can be very steep sided and narrow at the base, or broad and flat. Many have bodies of water such as rivers and lakes at their lowest elevation points. Valleys are formed through two major geologic processes. Narrow, steep, V-shaped valleys are formed by rivers by their erosional effect of cutting through rock. Valleys with rivers in them generally start out steeper at higher elevations, then broaden and flatten as they approach the ocean. Mountains or hills that are uplifting due to mountain-building processes may increase the rate of erosion and create steeper sided valleys or canyons. More easily eroded materials such as sandstone may also result in faster erosion and deeper canyons.

Rivers that are left to their natural course frequently meander and flood, creating broad, flat flood plains or marshes near their mouths, and river deltas where they deposit sediment as they slow down upon entering an ocean or a lake. The soil in these areas is quite fertile and is good for farming.

Wide, flat, U-shaped valleys were frequently formed by glaciers, which have since melted, often leaving behind large boulders or ridges of rounded rocks known as glacial moraines. The soil type in these areas is often composed of glacial till, which are unsorted sediments carried by the glaciers and left behind after melting. This is composed of silts, sands, gravels, and boulders of varying sizes. Some very large valleys may have once been inland seas or lakes.

Mountains are formed due to processes related to plate tectonics. These include collision of continental plates, subduction of oceanic plates beneath continental plates, and volcanic activity related to hot spots.

Hills are formed through a variety of different processes. Glacial activity on a large scale can create irregular scours, creating rolling hills and depressions. Glaciers can also leave behind large deposits known as moraines that appear as hills. Mountains can be uplifted and eroded away, leaving behind large, rounded batholiths. Wind erosion and subsequent deposition can also create hills or dunes.

Plateaus are flat, elevated areas with steep sides, which encompass very large areas of Earth's surface. Plateaus may be formed through repeated volcanic action, when layer after layer of lava spreads out thinly over a large area to create a flat surface. Plateaus with steep sides may be left behind when other areas erode around them or when a river cuts a steep canyon or valley along its edge. Plateaus may be formed in areas that are being geologically uplifted.

Plains are broad, flat areas usually low in elevation. Coastal plains occur along the seacoast and rise gently to the foothills of the nearest mountain range. These coastal plains often extend out into the ocean and the continental shelf. Changes in sea level or changes in land elevation (through uplifting or subsidence) may change the area of coastal plains and either submerge or uplift them over geologic time. Plains may be extended by erosion of nearby mountains or hills and deposits formed at river mouths or through flooding. Inland plains may be found at higher altitudes but are still generally broad and flat over large areas.

Ice sheets and **glaciers** are landforms of snow and ice that cover extensive regions at the poles and in mountain areas. These landforms contain most of the freshwater on Earth, which is deposited in cold, mountainous and polar regions, and forms relatively permanent landforms. Glaciers and ice sheets move very slowly, and are replenished each year in the upper elevations and lost each year at the lower elevation margin, often where the glacier meets the ocean. Polar ice increases in area each winter and shrinks in the summer. Both ice sheets and glaciers are diminishing in size worldwide because of global warming.

Coastal landforms include estuaries, bays, spits and bars, peninsulas, headlands, fjords, and islands.

Estuaries are locations where rivers meet the ocean, and freshwater and saltwater mix. Natural river mouths may be characterized by deposition of sediment and multiple channels of freshwater running out to the ocean in a fan-shaped pattern. Estuaries are frequently biologically rich and may support marshes, wetlands, and swamps.

Bays are areas along the coast where wave action has eroded sections of the coastline and created a circular indentation, which becomes relatively sheltered from the elements. Rocky areas along the shoreline that erode less easily remain as **headlands** or outcroppings, sometimes with arches, stacks, or other fanciful shapes. A **peninsula** is a headland that sticks out into the water, and is surrounded by water on all but one side.

A **spit** or **bar** is a long beach that extends out into the water and is formed by coastal erosion and deposition processes. Sand is eroded from areas up the coast and then deposited in a location where the current slows down. Bars may also be formed at the mouths of rivers where they slow down and meet the sea, or in rivers in places where the current slows down.

Fjords are areas where the coastline has become inundated, either due to a rise in sea level or subsidence of the land. The beach areas are lost and the coastline rises steeply from the sea.

Islands are formed through a wide variety of processes. **Barrier islands** may be formed through longshore transport and deposition of sand, erosion of the landward end of spits or peninsulas, or as remnants of a former river delta. **Coastal islands** can be formed through erosion of softer coastal materials, leaving behind harder, rocky areas unconnected to the mainland. Some islands are formed by rivers splitting and flowing around rocky areas, then reconnecting downstream. **Continental islands,** such as Greenland and other islands north of Canada, are elevated portions of the North American continent surrounded by submerged areas. **Oceanic islands** are formed through volcanic activity at hot spots, such as the Hawaiian Islands, or near subduction zones, such as Japan.

Skill 5.4   Evaluate the function and benefits of Earth-observing systems (e.g., Landsat, Topex, aircraft, balloons).

Earth-observing systems range from photographs taken by aircraft or astronauts in space to satellites recording infrared or microwave radiation. A few specific types of systems are discussed here.

Landsat: The Landsat program, a joint mission of NASA and the USGS, is a series of satellite missions to collect information about Earth as viewed from space. The Landsat program has greatly aided the science of remote sensing. The program has been collecting and archiving photographs of Earth since the early 1970s, providing an opportunity for scientists to view and evaluate changes in Earth's surface over time.

TOPEX/Poseidon: The goal of the TOPEX/Poseidon mission was to map ocean surface topography using satellites. The mission, which ran from 1992 until 2006 and was a joint NASA/Centre National d'Etudes Spatiales (CNES) venture, resulted in extensive data on sea level, global ocean topography, seasonal changes of ocean currents, phenomena such as El Niño and La Niña, the tides, and much more.

Aerial photography: Aerial photographs are taken of Earth's surface by airplanes. They can be used by cartographers when preparing maps, and are also valuable for identifying and interpreting changes in surface conditions. They provide an excellent method of identifying changes to an area over time, such as land-use changes or habitat destruction.

Balloons: Special types of balloons are also used in Earth-observations. Weather balloons are released into the atmosphere carrying instruments to collect and transmit data on weather conditions as far as 125 miles away and 100,000 feet in altitude. Weather balloons provide valuable data about above-ground weather conditions, and are an important source of information for forecast models.

Skill 5.5   Identify the applications of remote sensing technologies used on Earth and in space science (e.g., magnetometry, seismic survey, ground-penetrating radar, high-resolution photography).

There are several different types of remote sensing technologies that are useful to Earth and space scientists. (See Skill 12.2 for a discussion of space exploration technology.)

Magnetometry: Magnetometry is a method of subsurface exploration that relies on the detection of variations in the magnetic field. This method is useful for identifying certain types of buried objects or structural features. Magnetometry is useful to identify subsurface locations that have undergone a measureable change in magnetic field due to past activities.

Seismic surveys: Seismic surveys use seismic waves to obtain data about subsurface features and structures. **Seismic refraction** relies on the fact that seismic waves travel at different speeds through different materials. In a seismic refraction survey, travel times of seismic waves that are refracted at the boundaries between different subsurface materials or structures are measured. The data collected on the differences in travel times can be used to map bedrock and certain subsurface structures. **Seismic reflection** measures the round-trip travel time of waves moving from the surface and reflected back again by the boundaries between geologic materials. Seismic reflection surveys are useful for determining the depth to a certain geologic feature, such as bedrock.

Ground-penetrating radar: Ground-penetrating works by sending pulses of high frequency radio waves into the ground. These waves reflect off buried materials and/or boundaries between geologic materials and structures and return to the surface. The time the round-trip takes is measured and used to create a three-dimensional picture of the subsurface environment. The technique can be used to locate subsurface pipes, tanks, concrete, sinkholes, geologic features, archaeological deposits, and more.

High-resolution photography: High resolution photography of Earth's surface has a variety of applications. For example, cartographers can use aerial photographs of areas to create maps. They can also be used to deduce changes to an area over time. Aerial photographs can reveal land use changes and/or habitat destruction in a given area over time. Aerial photography can also be useful to land-use planners and the military.

COMPETENCY 6.0   KNOWLEDGE OF THE SCOPE AND MEASUREMENT OF GEOLOGIC TIME

Skill 6.1   Identify appropriate methods of absolute and relative dating for given situations.

Relative Dating

Relative dating techniques reveal the age relationships of rocks to one another—which formed first, second, third, and so on. Relative dating techniques are most appropriate where materials for absolute dating are unavailable. These techniques rely on some basic principles and rules of geology:

Principle of Uniformitarianism: Processes that are happening today also happened in the past.

Law of Original Horizontality: Layers of sediment are originally laid down flat. Sedimentary layers that are still flat can be assumed not to have undergone any deformation. This law is useful in areas of sedimentary rocks.

Law of Superposition: In a sequence of undeformed sedimentary rocks, the oldest is at the bottom and the youngest is at the top. This law is only applicable to sedimentary rocks.

Principle of Cross-Cutting Relationships: A rock is older than any other rock or structure that cuts across it. This principle can help reveal the relationship among igneous, metamorphic, and sedimentary rocks.

Principle of Biologic Succession: Certain fossils, called index fossils, correspond to particular periods of time. Fossils appear and disappear periodically, providing a geologic time yardstick. This technique is useful only where appropriate fossils are found.

Absolute Dating

Absolute dating involves quantifying the date of a given material in years.

Dendrochronology: Dendrochronology uses tree ring growth to date events and conditions of the recent past. This was an early technique used in absolute dating. By measuring the width of the tree rings and counting the number of rings, a scientist could make an approximation of the climatology of the area and how old the tree was when it died. . Tree-ring indexes have been developed allowing dendrochronologists to date events and climatic conditions going back several thousand years.

Varves: Varves are sedimentary layers seasonally deposited in a lake. Counting varves can provide information as to the age of the deposit. Maximum dating range limited to the past 20,000 years.

Both dendrochronology and counting varves are relatively inaccurate methods.

Radiometric dating: The most accurate method of absolute dating, this technique measures the decay of naturally occurring radioactive isotopes. Radioactive elements decay into stable daughter elements, and each element has its own unique **half-life**. The half-life is the time it takes for half of the original, or parent isotope, to decay into its daughter product. This is the basis for radiometric dating. Once the half-life is established, the amount of time the decay has been occurring can be determined by measuring the ratio of the amount of radioactive element to the amount of its stable decay product.

Carbon-14 dating is a method commonly used to get an absolute date on organic material. The dating process compares the ratio of carbon-14 to carbon-12 in an object. Since the decay occurs at a known rate, it is very predictable and can be used as a clock standard. However, carbon-14 decays quickly and can only be used to date organic compounds less than 40,000 years old.

Applications of Radiometric Dating:

Radioactive isotope dating is a relatively new invention. Prior to its invention, geologists relied upon relative dating methods. Radioactive isotopes are good for dating rock units because they are common in igneous rocks, some metamorphic rocks, and occasionally in sedimentary rocks such as sandstone. However, the presence of the isotope in a sedimentary rock can tell us how old the material itself is, but not when the sedimentary unit was laid down. To determine the age of sedimentary units, scientists try to date layers above and below. Thus, dating of sedimentary rocks uses a combination of absolute and relative dating methods.

Radiometric Isotopes Commonly Used in Absolute Dating

Parent Isotope	Stable Daughter Product	Currently Accepted Half-Life Values
Uranium-238	Lead-206	4.5 billion years
Uranium-235	Lead-207	704 million years
Thorium-232	Lead-208	14.0 billion years
Rubidium-87	Strontium-87	48.8 billion years
Potassium-40	Argon-40	1.25 billion years
Samarium-147	Neodymium-143	106 billion years

Fission Track Dating

Fission track dating is an alternative method that doesn't rely on parent-daughter techniques. Instead, it is based on counting the scars caused by the collision of atoms. However, because the method is relatively new, it is controversial and not completely accepted by all scientists.

Skill 6.2   Apply the law of original horizontality, the principle of superposition, and the principle of cross-cutting relationships to interpret geologic cross sections.

For an explanation of the law of original horizontality, the principle of superposition, and the principle of cross-cutting relationships, see Skill 6.1.

Geologists interpret the order of physical events or the geologic history of an area by observing and creating standardized diagrams of rocks. In most areas rock formations are covered by vegetation or development, or are underground, so geologists must extrapolate based on rocks that are visible at or above the ground surface, or use information gained by drilling or geophysical exploration.

Geologic cross sections are used to create a side view of a slice through a section of the crust. Using the geologic principles and laws discussed in Skill 6.1, it is possible to deduce the age relationship of rocks and structures in a given geologic cross section. A brief example is given using the image below.

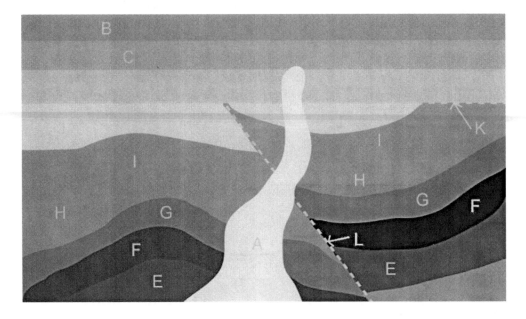

(from http://www.learner.org/courses/envsci/visual/img_lrg/geologic_crosssection.jpg)

Using knowledge of geologic laws and principles, it is possible to interpret this hypothetical geologic cross section as follows:

- Using the principle of superposition, we can determine that E is the oldest labeled sedimentary bed, followed by F, G, H, I, and J.
- Based on the law of original horizontality, we can determine that beds E through J became deformed (folded) sometime after they were laid down.
- After those beds were deposited and deformed, they were cut by fault L. Using the principle of cross-cutting relationships, we can determine that fault L is younger than beds E through J.
- Again using the principle of cross-cutting relationships, we can determine that erosional event K is younger than beds E through J as well as fault L.
- After the erosional event, beds D, C, and B were laid down, in that order (law of superposition).
- The volcanic intrusion, A, can be interpreted to be younger than any bed or structure it penetrates (principle of cross-cutting relationships).
- Based on this diagram, it is impossible to say if intrusion A or sedimentary bed B is the youngest feature, since their relationship is not clear.

Skill 6.3 **Identify major events in Earth's history (e.g., mass extinctions, evolution of plants, development of an oxygen-rich atmosphere).**

Eon	Era	Period	Epoch	Time	Events
Precambrian	Hadean			4.5 to 3.8 bya	formation of the solar system
	Archaean			3.8 to 2.5 bya	first life appears (bacteria), oxygen begins to be released into the atmosphere
	Proterozoic			2.5 bya to 543 mya	appearance of stable continents, first fossils of living organisms, appearance of eukaryotic cells, oxygen build-up in atmosphere, first animals
Phanerozoic	Paleozoic	Cambrian		543 to 490 mya	appearance of most of the major groups of animals—Cambrian Explosion,
		Ordovician		490 to 443 mya	most of world's land part of supercontinent Gondwana, diverse marine invertebrates, evidence that plants invaded land, mass extinctions at end of Ordovician
		Silurian		443 mya to 417 mya	stabilization of climate, melting of glaciers, rise in sea level, first coral reefs, major evolution of fishes, earliest fossils of vascular plants
		Devonian		417 to 354 mya	appearance of first land-living vertebrates, rapid diversification of fish, land divided into three major continental masses
		Carboniferous		354 to 290 mya	beginnings of coal formation, appearance of amniote egg, mild temperatures, collision of Laurasia and Gondwana
		Permian		290 to 248 mya	huge mass extinction at end of Permian (especially marine life), fern-like plants shift to gymnosperms, appearance of modern conifers, Pangaea,
	Mesozoic	Triassic		248 to 206 mya	evolution of dinosaurs, recovery/changes related to Permian mass extinction
		Jurassic		206 to 144 mya	dinosaurs dominate land, abundance of marine life, appearance of first birds
		Cretaceous		144 to 65 mya	new dinosaurs appear, modern insect, mammal, and bird groups, first flowering plants, breakup of Pangaea, massive extinction at end of Cretaceous

					wiped out the dinosaurs
	Cenozoic	Tertiary	Paleocene	65 to 54.8 mya	sea level drop, mammals flourish, continental landmasses largely seperated,
			Eocene	54.8 to 33.7 mya	high global temperatures, much precipitation, modern ungulates became prevalent mammals
			Oligocene	33.7 to 23.8 mya	appearance of first elephants with trunks, early horses, appearance of many grasses, global marine regression
			Miocene	23.8 to 5.3 mya	appearance of kelp forests and grasslands, changes in ocean circulation, buildup of Antarctic ice cap, African-Arabian plate joined to Asia
			Pliocene	5.3 to 1.8 mya	global cooling, major spread of grasslands and savannas, rise of long-legged grazers, Panamanian land bridge appears, more ice accumulation at the poles
		Quaternary	Pleistocene	1.8 mya to 10,000 years ago	presence of biological forms very much like modern types, also presence of large land mammals and birds extinct today, ice ages, evolution and expansion of *Homo sapiens*, extinction of large Pleistocene mammals,
			Holocene	10,000 years ago to present	relatively warm interglacial period, "Age of Man"

Skill 6.4   Identify major events in Florida's geologic history, including sea-level changes.

Formation of Present-day Florida

The landmass that would later become Florida originally formed along the northwest portion of present-day Africa as a result of volcanic activity and the deposition of marine sediments during the early Ordovician (about 530 million years ago). During the late Carboniferous (300 million years ago), the Florida platform was wedged between what are now present-day North and South America and Africa. As Pangaea split up, the Florida platform was eventually dragged toward its current location with the North American continent.

Sea Level Changes

During the early Cenozoic, the Florida platform was submerged beneath the Tethys Sea. While the platform was submerged, the skeletons of billions of marine invertebrates were deposited, building up the limestone platform that forms much of Florida's bedrock.

As sea levels rose and fell through time, areas of the platform experienced erosion and deposition of sediments. Freshwater runoff also began to dissolve bedrock, creating karst landforms such as sinkholes and caves.

During the last Ice Age, as sea level fell, Florida's land area was three times what it is today.

Florida's Fossil Record

Florida's fossil record records the sudden appearance of terrestrial fossils previously found only in South America, providing supporting evidence for the Great American Interchange—a mass migration of plants and animals between North and South America during the Pliocene (2.3 million years ago). This migration was made possible by the emergence of the Isthmus of Panama, which formed a land bridge.

Florida's fossil record records the sudden appearance of terrestrial fossils previously found only in South America, providing supporting evidence for the Great American Interchange—a mass migration of plants and animals between North and South America during the Pliocene (2.3 million years ago). This migration was made possible by the emergence of the Isthmus of Panama, which formed a land bridge.

Also preserved in Florida's fossil record is evidence of the extinction of the large terrestrial mammals. These mammals were wiped out by paleoindians, who arrived in Florida toward the end of the last ice age.

Skill 6.5   Interpret fossils and geologic evidence to reconstruct Earth's history.

Fossils

Paleontology is the study of past life based on fossil records and their relation to different geologic time periods. The distribution of fossils at different times in the geologic record provides an understanding of what lived where and where, and helps paleontologists interpret important events in Earth's history.

When organisms die, they often decompose quickly or are consumed by scavengers, leaving no evidence of their existence. However, occasionally some organisms are preserved; the remains or traces of the organisms from a past geological age embedded in rocks by natural processes are called fossils. They are very important for the understanding the evolutionary history of life on Earth as they provide evidence of evolution and detailed information on the ancestry of organisms.

Petrification is the process by which a dead animal gets fossilized. For this to happen, a dead organism must be buried quickly, to avoid weathering and decomposition. When the organism is buried, the organic matter decays. The mineral salts from the mud (in which the organism is buried) will infiltrate into the bones and gradually fill up the pores. The bones will harden and will then be preserved as fossils. If dead organisms are covered by wind-blown sand, and if the sand is subsequently turned into mud by heavy rain or floods, the same process of mineral infiltration may occur. Besides petrification, the organisms may be well-preserved in ice, in hardened resin of coniferous trees (amber), in tar, in anaerobic acidic peat. Fossilization can sometimes be a trace, an impression of a form (e.g. leaves and footprints).

The horizontal layers of sedimentary rocks are called *strata*, and each layer may contain fossils. The oldest layer is the one at the bottom of the pile. Therefore, fossils found in this layer are the oldest and this is how paleontologists determine the relative ages of these fossils.

Some organisms appear in only a few layers, which indicates that they lived only during that period and then became extinct. Such "index fossils" can be used to date geologic materials in other locations where they are found. The sudden disappearance of a wide variety of fossils indicates a mass extinction; the sudden appearance of a wide variety of fossils indicates rapid diversification. A succession of animals and plants can also be seen in fossil records, which supports the theory that organisms tend to progressively increase in complexity.

According to fossil records, some modern species of plants and animals are found to be almost identical to the species that lived in ancient geological ages. They are existing species of ancient lineage that have remained unchanged morphologically, and may be physiologically unchanged as well. Hence, they are called "living fossils." Some examples of living fossils are tuatara, nautilus, horseshoe crab, gingko and metasequoia.

Geologic Evidence

Geologic evidence also provides information about Earth's history. For example, it is possible to correlate areas with evidence of past glaciations and similar fossil assemblages across the Atlantic, which provides supporting evidence for plate tectonics, indicating the areas were once joined and have since spread apart.

On a smaller scale, the geologic features of an area can reveal much about the area's history. Ancient river channels, sand dunes, faults, and folds can all be preserved in the rock record. The presence of mountains indicates an ancient orogeny. Volcanic rock reveals that the area was once volcanically active. The discovery of marine rocks on land could indicate that the area was once covered by the sea, or that tectonic forces have uplifted marine strata. The existence of glacial deposits means the area at one time was covered with ice. Analysis of rocks can even provide information about ancient climates. Geologists can use such evidence preserved in the geologic record of an area to determine its past history.

(See also Skill 6.1, section on relative dating for information on geologic principles and laws.)

COMPETENCY 7.0   **KNOWLEDGE OF THE CHARACTERITICS AND MANAGEMENT OF EARTH'S RESROUCES**

Skill 7.1   Identify characteristics of renewable and nonrenewable resources.

Natural resources: naturally created commodities critically important or necessary to human life and civilization. The term natural resource can also include the total quantity of a given resource commodity on Earth, both discovered and undiscovered.

A major source of contention in our modern society is the proper use and conservation of our natural resources. Although most people automatically think of coal, oil, iron, and other minerals when they think of natural resources, the definition also includes other often overlooked resources such as forests, soil, water, air, and land.

Our natural resources are classified into two broad categories: **renewable resources** and **nonrenewable resources**.

Renewable resource: a resource that is capable of replenishment or regeneration on a human timescale. Example: Forests and water.

Nonrenewable resource: a resource that, once exhausted, is not capable of replenishment or regeneration on a human timescale. Example: Petroleum and minerals.

With the exception of certain commodities (gold, silver, and salt), humans have historically given little thought to the concept of managing resources. The supply of every conceivable resource seemed boundless. Vast forests covered large parts of the planet, ensuring a seemingly ample supply of wood for heating and construction. Ore deposits, although less accessible than the forests, were plentiful.

At first, our natural **reserves**, the quantity of a resource material that has been discovered and is economically or technologically recoverable, kept pace with the demand.

However, as the population increased and civilization advanced, becoming increasingly technologically dependent, the demand on our natural resources soared.

More important, the per capita consumption of resources has dramatically increased. With an increased standard of living, comes the specter of increased individual consumption and strong dependence on machinery and manufactured goods.

Skill 7.2   Evaluate management strategies for renewable and nonrenewable resources.

Renewable Resource Concerns

We have a watery planet. Unfortunately, a large percentage (97%) of the water is not fit for human consumption or agricultural use due to high salinity.

Plants and animals (including humans) require water for survival. In fact, statistics show that every person in the United States uses 300 liters of water, and when industrial uses are included, that number soars to roughly 5,000 liters per day, per person.

Pollution poses the severest threat to the water supply. Organic wastes are produced by both humans and animals. If left untreated, these wastes along with the wastes from food treatment plants can enter the waterways and upset the ecological balance.

As the wastes decay they consume oxygen in the water, depriving aquatic life forms of oxygen, or causing algae blooms which further deplete the oxygen supply, eventually turning some water anoxic.

Another danger is the poisoning of the food chain through pesticides and fertilizers, or with high concentrations of heavy metals carried into the water supply through runoff from farmlands, factories, and mine tailings.

Pollution also affects our air. The uncontrolled burning of fossil fuel hydrocarbons and high-sulfur content coals pose severe health risks, especially to the very young and very old. Smog alerts are routine in many of the major metropolitan areas, and in Mexico City, air pollution is reaching a critical level.

Forestry management is another area of concern. As our population grows, the demand for lumber and wood products has grown exponentially. Increased urbanization has claimed once vast tracts of forests, replacing them with concrete paving and closely packed structures.

This same drive toward urbanization also affects our soil. Arable farmland is shrinking as the pressure to develop home and commercial sites increases. Of the approximately 15 billion hectares of dry land on Earth, only 2 billion are suitable for agriculture. If the same land is used year after year, there is a definite danger of soil exhaustion as vital nutrients are depleted.

Farmland is not the only victim of urbanization. Grazing lands for our cattle and other domesticated animals are also shrinking, and as a consequence, many of the remaining areas are being overgrazed. The danger of overgrazing lays in the non-availability of sufficient pasturage for the animals and the loss of top cover for the soil, which is then left vulnerable to erosion.

Nonrenewable Resource Concerns

The key focus in nonrenewable resources is the every-increasing demand for energy. The concern with regard to nonrenewable resources is that once they are depleted, they are permanently gone.

Despite a finite supply of fossil fuels and radioactive fuels such as uranium, the demand for energy continues to increase at a high rate. At our present rate of consumption, there are only 28 years of petroleum reserves left, and uranium reserves are estimated at depletion in 40 years.

To try to alleviate this predictable energy gap, scientists are exploring new methods of recovering additional fuels from once economically unfeasible sites, and researching alternative energy sources.

See Skill 7.4 for a discussion of alternative energy sources.

Addressing the Issues

Our increasing population, urbanization, and dependence on technology are the key factors that drive the rapid consumption of our resources.

How long our natural resources will last depends on future demand and willingness on the part of governments to efficiently manage their energy needs and resources.

Likewise, industry must be more deeply involved by modifying existing, or developing new, techniques and procedures to effectively utilize our natural materials.

Unfortunately, natural resources are not evenly distributed throughout Earth, and political considerations have, to date, hampered cooperation of conservation efforts and development of alternative energy sources on a global scale.

As grim as the projected shortfalls may seem, there is some hope. There is a growing awareness of the problems we face and although not usually coordinated on a global scale, some countries are taking steps to address the issues.

Better agricultural techniques to prevent soil depletion, reclamation of waterways, banning use of chemicals damaging to the atmosphere, recycling plastics and metals, and seeking alternative energy sources are all examples of ongoing initiatives to ensure resources for future generations.

Skill 7.3   Assess the use and management of Florida's geologic, marine, and environmental resources.

Geologic resources

The map below shows the primary mineral resources of Florida. Florida has few oil and gas deposits onshore, but does have other important mineral resources.

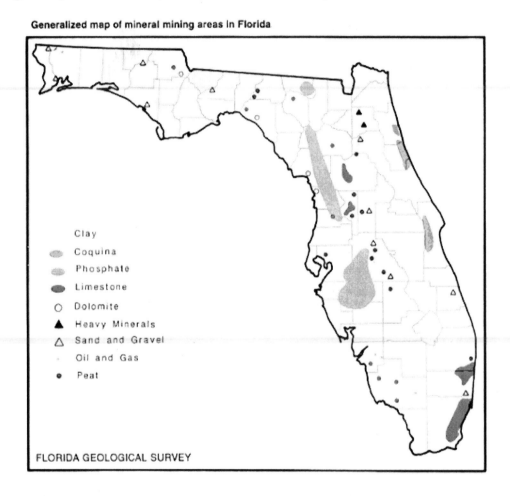

Generalized map of mineral mining areas in Florida

Clays are used to manufacture cement and construction materials, light weight aggregate, kitty litter, and other absorbent materials. Coquina, limestone, and dolomites are mined and crushed to prepare crushed rock for roadbeds, construction, manufacturing of concrete and cement, rip-rap, and fertilizer. Phosphate minerals are also used as fertilizers and in a wide variety of commercial products.

Heavy metals, such as titanium, zirconium, and rare Earth minerals are used in the aerospace, military, chemical, petroleum, and metal manufacturing industries. Sand and gravel are mined for construction of roadbeds, fill material, asphalt, and concrete, and some sand is used as an abrasive. Peat is farmed for horticultural uses, primarily in the Everglades. Relatively small oil and gas deposits are found in southwest Florida and in the extreme west panhandle.

Water resources

Drinking water in Florida comes primarily from a groundwater aquifer called the Floridian aquifer, which is confined in some areas and unconfined in others. Because of abundant rainfall and the highly permeable rocks that underlie much of Florida, the Floridian aquifer contains a vast amount of fresh water (2.2 quadrillion gallons). While extremely important as a source of drinking water, the water table is shallow and unconfined in many areas, and therefore highly vulnerable to pollution. In most areas of the state, there is only a thin layer of vegetation and soil above limestone, sand, and gravel aquifers. Aquifers in southern areas of the state may also be saline due to intrusion of ocean water and low elevations.

In the central, northern, and panhandle areas of the state, where carbonate rocks are near the surface, numerous freshwater surface springs exist, along with karst features such as caves and sinkholes. Increasing nitrate concentrations in groundwater and springs from agriculture and intrusion of saline water are both concerns that are currently being addressed. The map below shows the locations of Florida's primary springs and wetlands.

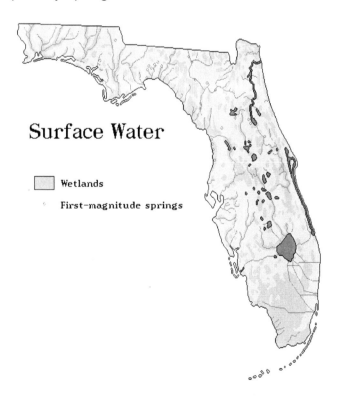

Environmental resources

The highest-quality wetlands in Florida are located within the Everglades, a unique wetland, which once encompassed the lower half of Florida. As can be seen from the map below, much of this area is less than 20 feet above sea level, and has been called a "river of grass." The building of roads, canals, and levees to support agriculture and development have altered the natural water flow pattern of the Everglades, leading to the loss of 50% of its wetland areas and unique habitats, as well as other ecological functions. The Comprehensive Everglades Restoration Plan is a long-term project by the Corps of Engineers and the South Florida Water Management District, along with many other partners, to restore the natural water flow of the Everglades and bring it back to health. It is thought that this may also help restore natural conditions offshore in the Florida Bay and the Keys.

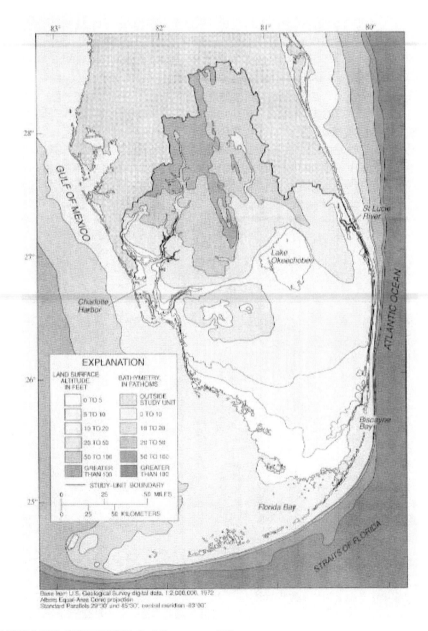

There are a wide variety of other important environmental landscapes in Florida as well. Because of its unique evolutionary history, nearly 8% of Florida's species are not found anywhere else on Earth, and the state is considered a global biological "hot spot" of biodiversity. Examples include cypress and hardwood swamps, which occur throughout the state and harbor many unique species of plants, rare birds, and mammals. The Everglades is home to several endangered bird species, as well as the endangered Florida panther. In upland areas of the central and northern portion of the state, longleaf and other pine forests host a variety of endangered birds and mammals, but are rapidly being lost to agricultural uses and other development. Temperate hardwood forests in the panhandle contain several unique trees and endemic plant species.

Marine resources

Florida's coastal ecosystems are also biologically diverse and unique. The Florida Keys are surrounded by tropical coral reefs, which provide habitat for an abundance of sea grass, invertebrates, fish, and shellfish. Many commercial and recreational species spawn and live in this habitat, including lobster, grouper, and snapper; aquarium species are also fished here. Nutrient pollution and sediments threaten this area, but restoration of the Everglades is intended to help remedy this problem. Bleaching of coral reefs has also been observed, but is as yet poorly understood.

Nearshore coastal areas provide seagrass habitat supporting shrimp, crab, scallop, and oyster fisheries. Mangrove swamps are found along the southwestern coastline, and support many endangered species of fish and birds, as well as the American crocodile and Florida manatee. Florida's Atlantic coastal dunes and beaches provide a globally important area for sea turtle nesting, as well as habitat for several endangered bird species, and endemic plants and rodents.

Skill 7.4   Compare various energy production technologies (e.g., fossil fuels, nuclear, solar) and their past, present, and future consequences to the environment.

Energy production technologies range from the burning of fossil fuels to harnessing of power from the sun and wind. Each method of generating energy has a unique history and its own set of benefits and challenges.

Fossil fuels—coal, oil, and natural gas—comprise more than 85% of the energy used in the United States. They are formed from the remains of animals and plants that lived hundreds of millions of years ago, and are considered a non-renewable resource because the supply is limited.

While fossil fuels have proved to be a reliable source of energy for thousands of years, their use is not without consequences. One of the main problems with the use of fossil fuels is the emissions that result when they are burned. Burning fossil fuels releases greenhouse gasses, possibly contributing to global warming. Particulate matter and other compounds released are responsible for air pollution and acid rain. Because fossil fuels are generally found below ground, they need to be extracted by mining or drilling. Water pollution, subsidence, land degradation, and spills are all possible side affects of extracting fossil fuels.

Another problem with fossil fuels is that the global supply is running out. Because the supply is limited, and population growth places an ever greater demand on energy resources, it is imperative that other, renewable sources of energy be developed and used.

Nuclear energy production relies on the harnessing of energy released by radioactive materials during nuclear fission. The process usually uses uranium-235 atoms, which are bombarded with neutrons. This bombardment causes the nuclei to split, emitting neutrons and heat energy. These released neutrons then strike other atoms, causing a chain reaction. An uncontrolled chain reaction would cause an explosion, so in a nuclear reactor the reaction is controlled using neutron-absorbing rods, allowing for a great deal of energy to be harnessed without an explosion. Because the supply of uranium is not unlimited, nuclear energy is also considered a non-renewable resource.

While nuclear power presents a "clean" energy source (one that does not emit greenhouse gases), it is not without problems. One drawback of nuclear power is the fact that it is extremely expensive to build and maintain safe nuclear reactors. Moreover, the potential consequences of a nuclear accident are significant. As the 1986 Chernobyl accident demonstrated, a nuclear accident has the potential to cause health risks to the public for years following the accident. Lastly, the radioactive waste created during the production of nuclear power also poses a disposal problem.

Renewable Resources

Solar energy involves using the energy provided by the Sun's rays to satisfy the energy needs of people. The most basic way of using solar energy, called *passive solar collection*, is by installing south-facing windows in a house. Sunlight heats the room and that heat then permeates throughout the home. This is especially effective in homes with good insulation and airtight construction. *Active solar collection* involves the use of specially constructed panels designed to collect and transfer solar energy. They are generally mounted on roofs, and can be used to provide hot water and heat homes. Solar energy provides a valuable energy source in the future, especially as the cost of non-renewable fuels continues to increase.

Potential drawbacks of solar energy include high start-up costs and a need for backup systems for use during cloudy days and/or at night.

Wind power is another form of renewable energy. It involves converting wind's mechanical energy into electricity using windmills or wind turbines. In areas with sufficient wind-speeds, the use of wind power is a cost-effective way to produce clean energy. In the future, wind-generated power is expected to increase as technology improves.

Wind-generated power relies on wind turbines, which some people find noisy or unpleasant to look at. Also, trees must be cleared and roads must be built to create wind energy facilities in undeveloped areas. Wind turbines are also responsible for killing many birds and bats.

Hydroelectric power is produced by the energy released by moving water. Waterwheels have long been used to grind grain and power machinery; today water power can be used to produce electricity. The production of hydroelectric power relies on the construction of huge dams. The reservoirs behind such dams store water, which can be released according to the need to produce electricity.

One problem with hydroelectric power is that sediment carried by a river will eventually fill up the reservoir behind a dam. It can also be difficult to locate an appropriate dam site. Additionally, dams change the nutrient and sediment flow of rivers, flood the upstream area, and alter the downstream ecosystem. Lastly, the construction of dams results in the loss of "wild" rivers. Most good dam sites have already been exploited; therefore, hydroelectric power production will probably not increase significantly in the future.

Tidal power involves the generation of electricity from the movement of the oceans. To harness the power of the tides, a dam is constructed across the mouth of a bay in an area with a large tidal range. The flow of the tides drives turbines and generators, producing electricity.

The use of tidal power relies on a specific set of conditions (narrow bay, high tidal range), so it is not practical along most of the world's coastlines. Therefore, tidal power will probably never play a significant role in global energy production. However, where the conditions are right, tidal power can offer a feasible clean energy option.

Geothermal energy is derived from natural underground sources of steam and hot water. Geothermal energy can be used to provide hot water as well as to produce electricity. Power plants may be constructed in geothermal areas to harness the heat energy and use it to drive turbines to create electricity.

Geothermal power plants have little impact on the environment; they emit only steam, do not require massive networks of underground pipes, and do not rely on the burning of non-renewable resources. However, because geothermal energy can only be produced in certain areas, it will probably never be a huge contributor to global energy production. In areas with geothermal activity, though, its use is expected to grow.

Biomass energy is derived from organic materials such as plants and animals. Biomass can be burned or converted to fuels such as methane gas, ethanol, or biodiesel.

While biomass burning provides a good way to cut down on organic waste products, it does release greenhouse gases, such as carbon dioxide, into the atmosphere. However, when crops are grown for use in biomass energy production, photosynthesis uses up a nearly equivalent amount of carbon dioxide. Additionally, clean burning technologies can significantly reduce the amount of emissions produced by the burning of biomass. Biofuels such as ethanol and biodiesel produce far fewer emissions than traditional transportation fuels, and provide a promising alternative for powering machinery and vehicles in the future.

Other potential future energy sources include **hydrogen fuel cells** and **nuclear fusion**. Hydrogen fuel cells rely on the burning of hydrogen fuel, and at present are not widely used. They offer a reliable source of clean energy, but currently are not cost-effective. Nuclear fusion relies on the joining of two nuclei, as opposed to the splitting of nuclei used in nuclear fission, and occurs at extremely high temperatures. Fusion would provide a clean, reliable source of energy if it can be developed; at present, the technology does not exist.

Skill 7.5   Identify the impact of humans on Earth (e.g., deforestation, urbanization, desertification, erosion, air and water quality, changing the flow of water).

Human beings have a significant impact on their environment. Everything from farming to construction alters the natural environment, often with far-reaching effects.

Deforestation is occurring at an alarming rate as population increases force people to clear ever more land for settlements. Forests are disappearing because of logging, fires, and the clearing of land for agriculture or cattle-grazing. Because trees naturally use carbon dioxide for photosynthesis, the loss of the world's forests has a direct impact on the greenhouse effect, potentially contributing to global warming. Also, as forests are destroyed, habitat is lost, decreasing Earth's biodiversity. Deforestation can also lead to erosion and flooding.

Urbanization is occurring globally as an increasing population leads to the growth of cities worldwide. Urbanization leads to an increase in paved areas, which reduces the amount of water that can infiltrate the land, resulting in more runoff and flooding. The construction of cities also results in the loss of natural areas and wildlife, as grasslands and forests are cleared for roads and homes. Cities also significantly increase pollution.

Desertification occurs when poor land use practices result in the expansion of desert-like conditions into other areas. Desertification is a significant problem in the world's arid regions, where farmland may be destroyed as desert conditions take over. The removal of natural vegetation (by plowing or grazing) to establish an agricultural are near a desert's edge is usually to blame.

Erosion is a natural activity that involves the removal and transport of sediments by the action of wind or water. Human activities, however, can cause or increase erosion. Mining, logging, poor agricultural processes, construction, and other activities may all increase erosion. Increased erosion may in turn damage agricultural areas, cause soil loss, clog rivers with sediment, and more.

Air and water quality are also affected by human activity. Air pollution can be caused by burning fossil fuels in factories or cars, the release of airborne pollutants from industrial and farming activities, and burning waste. Air pollution can lead to an increase in global warming, as well as directly affect human health when people breathe in pollutants. Water quality is affected when pollutants are discharged directly into water sources, or when they are carried by runoff from the land surface. Damaged water quality can make drinking water unsafe, cause fish to become contaminated, and destroy aquatic ecosystems.

Human activity also affects aquatic ecosystems when dams are built. Dams flood upstream areas, permanently altering upstream ecosystems. Furthermore, because dams withhold sediment, downstream ecosystems are altered as well; the cold, clear water found downstream of a dam lacks nutrients, which in turn affects the local wildlife. Controlling natural flooding events can also have far-reaching effects. For example, the Mississippi River's periodic natural flooding was responsible for supplying sediment to the floodplain. Because levees now contain these floods, sediment remains in the channel and rushes out to sea. The coastal area is therefore starved of sediment, and the subsiding delta is shrinking because its sediment supply is no longer replenished.

COMPETENCY 8.0   **KNOWLEDGE OF OCEANS AND COASTAL PROCESSES**

Skill 8.1   **Identify the characteristics of ocean basins, continental shelves, and coral reefs.**

Ocean basins: The world's ocean basins are not simply flat, featureless depressions filled with water. Rather, ocean basins display a vast array of topographic features and unique landforms. The continental shelf (shallow, flat area), slope (steep stretch connecting shelf to ocean floor), and rise (large, gentle slope of deposited sediments) mark the transition from land to ocean basin. V-shaped submarine canyons cut into the continental slope to great depths in various locations, often associated with major rivers. The ocean floor itself is made up of a relatively thin (average 5 km thick) layer of basalt. Thousands of volcanoes dot the ocean floor, and the mid-ocean ridge system runs through each ocean basin. In areas of active convergence, deep trenches exist, generally in areas of ocean-continent convergence.

Continental shelves: The continental shelf is a relatively shallow landmass, extending from the edge of most continents out into the ocean. The continental slope marks the transition from land to ocean, and it is here that the ocean truly begins.

Coral reefs: A coral reef is actually a consolidation of living animals. The corals go through stages of development:

     Larval stage: The coral is mobile and swims around.
     Adult stage: The coral attaches itself to a rock and remains there for the rest of its life. The coral feeds from its tentacles. When the coral dies, new corals build upon the shell of the dead coral, and the buildup of millions of coral into colonies creates huge reefs. However, only the outer layer of coral on the reef is alive. Coral have specific conditions that must be met for their survival and growth:

     1. Warm water: The coral's shell is composed of calcium carbonates that are more plentiful in warm waters. In cold water, the carbonates go into solution.
     2. Light: Coral has a symbiotic relationship with photosynthetic algae. If the algae disappear, the coral dies. This is called coral bleaching. Consequently, coral are only found in clear water, and usually only to a depth of 50 feet. They can't survive in heavily sedimented areas, as the water is too murky.

Types of Reefs

Fringing reef: coral that live along the shoreline and are connected to the landmass.

Barrier reef: coral that stay offshore and do not touch the land's surface. In deep water, the coral grows upward in a tall column. Only the top layer within 50 feet of the surface is alive.

Atoll: a coral island with a central lagoon. Atolls originally form as fringing reefs around small islands. If the central island is eroded, or subsides, the coral reef is left behind. Atolls are very common in the Pacific Ocean. Examples include Diego Garcia in the Indian Ocean and Midway Island in the Pacific Ocean.

Skill 8.2   Identify the geologic features of coastal geomorphic structures (e.g., barrier islands, estuaries, sandbars, capes, deltas, coral reefs).

Barrier islands: Barrier islands are located parallel to the mainland, separated by estuaries, bays, and/or lagoons, on a gently sloping continental shelf. These islands provide protection to the mainland from the brunt of ocean waves. They are typically wave straightened and are dynamic environments, as they are constantly being shaped and reshaped, eroded and deposited. Their formation depends on sand supply, wave energy, and tidal fluctuations. Barrier Islands make up 80% of the U.S. East Coast.

Estuaries: An estuary is a semi-enclosed coastal body of water with one or more rivers or streams flowing into it. It has an open connection to the sea, making its water part fresh and part salt (brackish). Estuaries are gentle areas and are known as hatcheries to many species. They have high rates of biological productivity.

Sandbars: A sandbar is a long, narrow area of deposited material (typically sand) within a body of water. This may be exposed, submerged, or both depending upon water heights associated with tides. They are created by a current (or waves) depositing the material which results in a localized shallowing of the water.

Capes: A cape is a narrow piece of land that juts out into the water. Examples: Cape Cod, the Cape of Good Hope.

Deltas: Deltas are created at the mouth of a stream where its load is deposited where the stream enters a quiet(er) body of water. Depending on where the stream empties into, different formations occur.

Coral reefs: See Skill 8.1.

Tombolos: Tombolos are beaches that connect part of the mainland (like a headland) to an island.

Baymouth bars: Baymouth bars form from sand across the mouths of bays.

Wave-cut platforms: The gentle rock slope that extends from the high-tide line to the low-tide line is called a wave-cut platform. It is created by the erosive activity of waves.

Spits: Spits are small extensions of beach, jutting out from in the direction of longshore drift.

Skill 8.3	**Analyze the movement of water through waves, tides, and currents.**

Waves

Ocean waves generally form as a result of wind blowing across the ocean surface. Waves move in an orbital pattern, causing an up and down motion. They have a forward or lateral motion only if moved by the wind, current, or tides. The depth of the wave where the energy is felt is equal to half of the wavelength. Below that depth, the water remains relatively calm. When a wave approaches the shore, and it "feels the bottom," the circular orbit action flattens out and becomes more elliptical. As the wavelength shortens, the wave steepens until it finally breaks, creating surf.

The individual water particles in a wave actually remain in the same place, only moving in a circle. It is the energy of the wave itself that is transferred forward to the next wave, until the wave reaches shore and breaks.

Tides

The periodic rise and fall of the liquid bodies on Earth are the direct result of the gravitational influence of the Moon and, to a much lesser extent, the Sun.

Tides are produced by the differences between gravitational forces acting on parts of an object. As shown in Newton's Universal Law of Gravitation, the gravitational effect of two bodies is mutually constant and depends largely on the distance and mass between the objects.

The side of Earth that faces the Moon is roughly 4,000 miles (6,400 km) closer to the moon than is Earth's center. This has the effect of increasing the Moon's gravitational attraction on Earth's oceans and landforms. Although the effect is so small on the mass of the landforms as to be invisible, the effect on the liquid parts is greater.

The Moon's gravitational effect causes a bulge to form on both sides of Earth. If we were able to view such subtle change from outer space, the affected waters would create an elliptical shape, compressing downward at the top and bottom of the planet and extending outward on the sides. This double-bulge effect causes the tides to fall and rise twice a day, and the time of the high and low tides is dependent on the phase of the moon.

Not all locations are uniformly affected. The tidal cycle at a particular location is actually a very complicated interaction of the location's latitude, shape of the shore, etc.

Example: The Bay of Fundy has a twice-daily tide that exceeds 12 meters, while the northern coast of the Gulf of Mexico only has one tidal cycle that seldom exceeds 30 centimeters rise and fall.

Because of its distance from Earth, the Sun's gravitational effect on tides is only half that of the Moon's. However, when the gravitational effects of both the Sun and Moon join together during a new moon and a full moon phase, when the Moon and Sun are aligned, the tidal effects can be extreme. During a new moon and a full moon, tidal effects are much more pronounced as the tidal bulges join together to produce very high and very low tides. These pronounced types of tide are collectively known as spring tides. During the first and third quarters of the moon phases, the Sun's effect is negligible and consequently, the tides are lower. These are neap tides.

Currents

A current is a body of water moving in a given direction. An ocean current refers to the directed flow of a parcel of ocean water. Currents can move water on a large or small scale. For example, ocean currents may move great volumes of water, affecting ocean and climate conditions on a global level. There are both surface currents and deep water currents. Some examples of ocean currents include:

Gulf Stream: The Gulf Stream is a strong, fast, warm, deep surface current in the Atlantic Ocean. It influences climate on the entire east coast of North America, as well as that of Western Europe.

California Current: This cool, slow, shallow current in the Pacific Ocean plays a role in creating fog along the California coast.

Global conveyor belt: The oceanic current that circles the globe and involves both deep and shallow water is known as the "global conveyor belt." This global current begins when seawater in the North Atlantic begins to freeze and form ice. When ice forms, the remaining water becomes saltier, and therefore denser. Sinking of this dense water causes surface water to move in to fill the void, initiating the global conveyor belt system. The deep water moves south, warms and rises, and then sinks again upon reaching the south polar region. This recharges the conveyor belt and keeps it moving. The current splits in several places and sections of it travel through each ocean basin, warming/rising and cooling/sinking according to the conditions.

Longshore current: Waves generally approach the shoreline at an angle. Because of this, water along the shoreline tends to flow parallel to shore in the same direction as the incoming waves. This flow is known as the longshore current, and works on a smaller scale than the global currents discussed above.

Skill 8.4   Identify the chemical, physical, and biological characteristics of seawater.

The Chemistry of the Oceans

We know that the outgassing and chemical weathering of rock washed into the seas cause the salinity of the ocean. However, what occurs to keep them from getting progressively saltier?

Although landlocked seas and some lakes may get saltier over time, the oceans do not. This is because the oceans have a chemical equilibrium- the proportion and amount of dissolved salts per unit volume of ocean are nearly even.

Essentially, ions are added to the ocean at a rate equal to those being removed. This is based on **residence time**: the length of time an element spends in the ocean.

The residence time for the additions of salts is balanced by the subtraction of minerals being bound into the sediments. However, the actual residence time of an element depends largely on its chemical activity.

Some elements, such as aluminum and iron, remain in the ocean for a relatively short time before incorporation in the sediment, while other elements such as chloride, sodium, and magnesium may linger in the water for millions of years.

The constant proportion of the elements in the seawater is due to **mixing**, the distribution of substances due to vigorous motion. In the oceans' case, this mixing is the result of the activity of the currents, with an estimated 1,000 year mixing cycle.

Elements in the ocean waters can be classified as either conservative or non-conservative constituents.

Conservative constituents are those elements that remain in constant proportion or change very slowly through time. Non-conservative constituents are those elements dissolved in seawater that are somehow tied to biological, seasonal, or short geological cycles.

Biological activity includes dissolved oxygen produced by plants, carbon dioxide produced by animals and humans, and silica and calcium compounds needed for plant and animal shells, or the nitrates and phosphates required for the production of proteins and other biochemicals.

The term seasonal is not tied to the climate. Instead, it refers to those elements that, by their nature, are rapidly absorbed into the sediment. Aluminum is such an element and it is relatively rare in seawater, because it is readily absorbed by clay sediment particles.

As the name implies, the geologic cycles are tied to geologic events that are relatively short in nature. These events may add a variety of elements to the seawater, some of which will have a long residence time, while others have a much shorter stay.

Dissolved Gasses in Seawater

Dissolved gasses in the seawater are very important to the marine life cycle. Surface gasses in the air easily dissolve in the ocean water. In terms of relative abundance, the major dissolved gasses are nitrogen, oxygen, and carbon dioxide. Nitrogen comprises around 48% of the dissolved gasses in the ocean. Living organisms need nitrogen to build proteins and other biochemicals necessary to sustain life. Nitrogen saturates the upper layers of the ocean.

Oxygen is the second most abundant gas in the ocean, with a content of around 36%. Although this percentage equates to only 6 parts per milligrams in each liter of seawater, oxygen in the water is as necessary in the ocean as it is in the air to sustain life, especially for those marine animals with gills. Not surprisingly, since most gilled marine life forms live in the surface layers, the majority of the oxygen in found there. It is largely produced by photosynthetic plant life that exchanges oxygen for carbon dioxide, and because of the abundance of marine plants, much more oxygen moves from the sea to the atmosphere, than from the atmosphere to the sea.

The third most abundant dissolved gas is carbon dioxide, comprising roughly 15% of the dissolved gasses in seawater. Carbon dioxide is very soluble in seawater and has an extremely high saturation level—1,000 times more than nitrogen or oxygen. However, this saturation level is seldom reached because of the high demand for carbon dioxide by marine plant life.

Fortunately for humans, much more CO_2 moves from the atmosphere to the ocean than the reverse direction. This is in part due to the fact that some of the carbon dioxide forms carbonate ions that are locked into minerals, sediments, and the exoskeletons and shells of marine creatures.

The pH Balance

Maintaining a proper balance between acids and bases is critical to sustaining life in the oceans. This balance is measured on the pH scale, which measures the concentration of hydrogen ions in a solution.

Pure water is considered neutral and is assigned a pH of 7.0. As the pH numbers decrease, the acidity increases. As the numbers go higher, the alkaline (base) properties increase.

Acid: a substance that releases a hydrogen ion in solution. An acidic solution has an excess of (H+) ions.

Base: a substance that combines with a hydrogen ion in solution. A base (alkaline) solution has an excess of hydroxide (OH-) ions.

The increase or decrease from a neutral pH is based upon the interactions of the hydrogen and hydroxide ions in the water. Hydrogen ions (H+) and hydroxide ions (OH-) are found in equal concentrations in pure water.

Seawater is not pure water. It actually is slightly alkaline with a pH of 7.4 to 8.4. Its median acidity is around 8.0-8.1.

This alkalinity is maintained despite the high concentrations of Carbon Dioxide because of the forms the CO_2 takes in the seawater. Although the CO_2 does combine with water to make carbonic acid (H_2CO_3), some of this acid breaks down to produce hydrogen ions (H+), bicarbonate ions (HCO_3-), and carbonate ions (CO_3^{2}-).

This breakdown results in the maintenance of the alkalinity, because as the pH of the ocean drops (increases in acidity), a reaction occurs which removes more H+ ions, returning the water to the proper balance.

Likewise, if the pH level increases (becomes more alkaline), more H+ ions are added to the water, once again maintaining the proper balance. This self-correcting feature of the seawater is called **buffering**.

Oceanic Depth and the pH Balance

Although the overall pH level of seawater is 8.0 to 8.1, the various water layers have different pH levels.
Surface layers are generally warmer and have and abundance of marine plant life. As the plants use the CO_2, the pH level changes because the exchange process removes H+ ions. This results in a pH level of approximately 8.5.

The middle and deep layers generally have more CO_2 present because of the lack of photosynthetic plant life (little sunlight penetration of these layers).

The layers' depth drives a change in pressure and temperature. The deeper you search, the more the pH balance shifts in an acidic direction. The water is still alkaline, but much less so than in the upper levels. The pH level below 15,000 meters is around 7.5.

At the very lowest depths (below 18,000 ft), bacteria consumes oxygen and produces hydrogen sulfide that can lower the pH to that of pure water, 7.0.

Salinity and Density

Salinity: the measure of the total concentration or amount of dissolved inorganic solids in water. Chloride (18%) and sodium (10%) are the most abundant solids in the water.

The mean temperature of the ocean is 3.5 °C.

The mean salinity is 35 ppt (parts per thousand).

Salinity changes the physical properties of water in four significant ways. Collectively, these four changes are referred to as water's Colligative Properties.

- Heat capacity of water decreases with a rise in salinity. Less heat is necessary to raise the temperature of seawater by l° than is required to raise the temperature of freshwater by an equal amount.
- Hydrogen bonding is disrupted by the concentration of salts in the water. The freezing point of seawater is lower than that of freshwater.
- Seawater evaporates more slowly than freshwater. The saline components tend to attract water molecules, causing the seawater to linger in the same circumstances under which freshwater evaporates.
- The osmotic pressure exerted on a biological membrane is different from that within the cells when salinity increases.

At 5,500 meters' depth, salinity remains extremely constant, and the current moves slowly with very little motion. There is a bigger density change in warmer water.

Water sinks until it reaches its potential **density**. Example: The waters off of the Straits of Gibraltar on the ocean side have almost no slope and the bottom is all rock. This is because of the cascade of high salinity, fast moving water out of the Mediterranean Sea.

Physical Layers of the Ocean

The layers of the ocean can be compared to the layers of an onion. Like an onion, the various layers overlap each other and meet at distinctive boundaries.

Central waters: Includes the shallow surface waters. These basically go around and around.

Intermediate waters: Can go both directions. Rarely found past a depth of 900 meters.

Deep water/bottom water: All the different layers of circulation are eventually tied together at the CDW (Circumpolar Deep Water), which has its origin in the North Atlantic.

Underneath the South Equatorial Current is a Subsurface Equatorial Counter-Current that flows eastward. Shaped much like a flat ribbon, the subsurface counter-current is only 200 meters thick and 2-3 degrees wide and it is located right on the geographical equator.

In general, the Deep Water Layer flows south, while the Antarctic Bottom Water layer flows north.

The Pacific water is much more uniform in temperature at depth. Likewise, the salinity index in the Pacific is very uniform. The Pacific waters take a long time to circulate in comparison to the Atlantic.

The Atlantic Ocean waters are much younger than that of the Pacific. The margin of overturn is greater than two times that of the Pacific. It's estimated that the Atlantic waters overturn every 600 years. The Pacific is on the order of 1500-1600 years.

The North Atlantic Deep and Bottom waters are major factors in ocean circulation because of the effect of the Gulf Stream. The Gulf Stream has higher salinity and density and a huge flow south after looping around Iceland. However, to really determine where the various layers begin and end, and how far they travel, we need to use Temperature-Salinity (TS) charts. To determine the fine, small changes, we must look at salinity.

Biological Layers of the Ocean

The ocean is commonly divided into five layers according to depth. Each layer has its own characteristics and a specific group of organisms reside there. The depth of water is key because photosynthesis requires solar energy. Therefore, the uppermost layer, where the light can penetrate, is where we can find phytoplankton. Phytoplankton are small, photosynthetic organisms which are the base of the oceanic food chain.

Epipelagic Zone – This layer extends from the surface to 200 meters (656 feet). It is in this zone that most of the visible light exists. The majority of plankton and fish are found here, as well as their predators (large fish, sharks, and rays).

Mesopelagic Zone - Extending from 200 meters (656 feet) to 1000 meters (3281 feet), the mesopelagic zone is also referred to as the twilight or midwater zone. Very little light penetrates here. Instead, most of the light observed is generated by bioluminescent creatures. A great diversity of strange fishes can be found here.

Bathypelagic Zone – This layer extends from 1000 meters (3281 feet) down to 4000 meters (13,124 feet). Here there is no penetration by solar light, so any light seen is in the form of bioluminescence. Most of the animals that live at these depths are black or red colored due to the lack of light. The water pressure at this depth is quite large, but a surprising number of creatures can be found here. Common inhabitants include fish, molluscs, jellies, and crustaceans. Sperm whales can dive down to this level in search of food.

Abyssopelagic Zone - Extending from 4000 meters (13,124 feet) to 6000 meters (19,686 feet), this zone has the least inhabitants. The water temperature is near freezing, and there is no light at all. Common organisms include invertebrates such as basket stars and squids. The name of this zone comes from the Greek meaning "no bottom", and refers to the ancient belief that the open ocean was bottomless.

Hadalpelagic Zone - This layer extends from 6000 meters (19,686 feet) to 10,000 meters (32,810 feet)- the sea floor. These areas are most often found in deep water trenches and canyons. In spite of the unimaginable pressures and cold temperatures, life can be found here. Generally, these include life forms that tolerate cool temperatures and low oxygen levels, such as starfish and tubeworms. The exception to this rule would be chemosynthetic communities living near deep-sea vents. These creatures create their own nutrients from carbon dioxide or methane released by the hot thermal vents. Chemosynthetic organisms then become prey to larger organisms. As such, chemosynthetic organisms are also primary producers and are at the bottom of the food chain, just like their photosynthetic friends, although they are at the opposite end of the ocean!

Skill 8.5 **Determine the causes and effects of surface currents, coastal upwelling, and density-driven (i.e., thermohaline) circulation.**

Two effects largely drive the patterns of surface water circulation in the world's oceans— wind related to pressure gradients and Coriolis forces. **Winds** blow from areas of high atmospheric pressure to areas of low atmospheric pressure. While these vary daily and seasonally, there are certain high and low pressure patterns that tend to occur on a large scale, globally speaking. As winds blow across the ocean from high to low pressure areas, they move the surface water in that direction. The speed of the surface water current is about 2-3% of the wind velocity.

Pressure gradients can be caused by variations in temperature and density. Cold water will tend to flow toward warmer equatorial areas, while warmer water will tend to flow toward polar regions.

$$\text{Pressure Gradient} = gi$$

Where g = gravity and i = the slope of the pressure gradient.

The **Coriolis force** is a term for the effect that Earth's rotation has on the wind's direction of travel. The wind is actually traveling in a straight line, but Earth is always rotating. Therefore, to an observer on the surface of Earth, the wind appears to travel along a curved path. Coriolis forces act in a perpendicular direction to the direction of travel, and are greater near the poles than at the equator. North of the equator, winds and associated surface currents travel in a clockwise direction, while south of the equator winds and associated surface currents travel in a counter-clockwise direction. At the equator, winds and surface currents travel in a straight line.

$$\text{Coriolis Effect} = fV$$

Where f = planetary vorticity and V = wind velocity. The depth of the ocean water that is affected by wind and Coriolis forces is about 50-200 m.

As winds blow parallel to a shoreline, Coriolis forces tend to push the winds and surface waters offshore. Deep water wells up to replace the displaced surface water and brings up rich nutrients for the marine food chain. This upwelling results in good fishing areas, such as in the Indian Ocean and along the coasts of Oregon and Peru/Chile. Upwelling also mixes surface water and deep ocean water, and helps drive large-scale ocean currents.

The next figure shows major surface currents of the ocean. Note the migration of colder water toward the equator and warmer water toward the poles, and the differing rotational directions of the gyres in the north and south hemispheres. These features have a strong effect on local climate. For example, the United Kingdom is much warmer than areas of Alaska that are at the same latitude, because of the warm Gulf Stream current that passes by the United Kingdom. As noted above, upwelling greatly affects local fisheries resources.

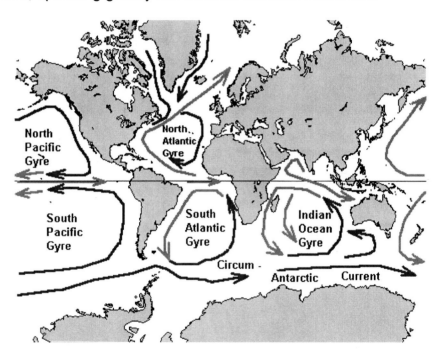

Another well-known effect of the interaction between winds and surface currents is the occurrence of El Niño and La Niña periods. In an El Niño period, trade winds along the equator weaken, and warm water is able to travel to the coast of South America. This reduces the upwelling of cold ocean water that normally occurs, and reduces fisheries resources. It also brings rain and warmer temperatures to coastal South America, and drought to Australia and the South Pacific. The effects of an El Niño period can be felt to lesser degrees in many other surrounding areas. La Niña periods, which generally follow El Niños, are characterized by colder than normal temperatures in the eastern Pacific and an increase in tropical cyclones in the Atlantic.

Equation of Motion (EOM)

The Equation of Motion addresses how water moves. Wind is the initial mover of water. The moving surface water couples with the water below it and moves the deeper water in varying degrees according to depth.

The general equation for force is: F=Ma (Force=mass times acceleration). However, for oceanography, the terms used are somewhat different and more specialized to the field.

Pressure Gradient = gi where g=gravity and i=the slope of the pressure gradient

Coriolis Effect =fV where f=planetary vorticity, and V=velocity.

Wind Stress = A d^2V where A=area, d^2 =diameter squared, and V=velocity.

Pressure Gradient: the difference between high and low pressure areas. The difference between the areas represents a range of varying high and low pressures. Changes in temperature and density occur within this area. The pressure gradient is a major player in determining ocean circulation. Example: The Gulf Stream is one of the strongest, most consistent ocean currents.

Ekman: The first scientist to try to solve the motion equation. However, he concentrated only on two of the EOM factors, Coriolis Effect and wind stress. Consequently, his predictions are somewhat flawed and are not truly useful for predicting ocean currents.

Other factors are needed to accurately predict the ocean current. Without them, according to Ekman, the whole ocean must go in the same direction. We know this is not true from observation of the ocean.

Ekman Spiral

The **Ekman spiral** is a theoretical model of the effect of wind blowing over water.

Because of the Coriolis effect caused by Earth's rotation and axial tilt (23.5° in relation to Polaris), a curvature effect is observed.

Wind drives surface water in a 45° direction to the right of the wind. The deeper you go, the less effect the surface water will have on the deeper water. However, for each succeeding layer of depth affected, they also twist 45° to the right of the previous layer.

Wind moving parallel to a shoreline results in up-swelling, and the Ekman spiral has the secondary use of predicting up-swelling.

The deep water up-swells to replace the displaced surface water and brings up rich nutrients for the marine food chain, resulting in good fishing areas. Example: The coasts of Oregon and Peru/Chile.

The Ekman Spiral also affects islands.

Inertial Motion

This model analyzes Coriolis effects and Acceleration only.

Cyclostrophic Flow

This model is composed of acceleration and pressure gradient only with very strong pressure gradients. The Coriolis effect is too small to contribute. Cyclostrophic flow has applications in predicting tornadoes.

Meander Motion

Encompasses acceleration, pressure gradient, and the Coriolis effect. Meander motion predicts that motion is essentially circular in nature.

Geostrophic Flow (Circular Gyres)

Pressure gradient and Coriolis effect based, the geostrophic flow model states that current flow parallel to a hill can be created in the ocean by changes in density, pressure, and temperature. A massive horizontal change in temperature also changes the density and pressure. For example, the Gulf Stream has one of the biggest horizontal pressure changes in the ocean. By plotting the temperature and salinity gradients, you can develop an idea of the pressure gradient. This allows you to determine the direction of flow of the current.

If the slope of the gradient goes to the right and upward, the flow is visualized as moving into the paper. If the slope of the gradient goes to the left and down, the flow is out of the paper. If the Coriolis effect and gravity are in balance, the flow goes straight and doesn't curve.

The Strommel Solution

Developed in 1948 by the oceanographer after which it is named, this is the major theory in ocean circulation. By developing a mathematical model to explain circulation, Strommel's theory revolutionized scientific prediction of ocean movement. Strommel approached his model in several steps.

He first combined the theories of geostrophic flow and the Ekman spiral and then used this combination in his attempts to prove that the maximum hill of water was near the Florida coast. Eventually, he showed why the Gulf Stream is where it is, and how strong it is in relation to the rest of the ocean.

Strommel's next step included using the pressure gradient and wind stress, but neglected the Coriolis effect, because his first model had presumed a non-rotating Earth. This time he modeled the ocean as being contained in a rectangular box. The intent of his model was still to show why the Gulf Stream is located where it is, by using a vertically integrated average for thickness and motion in the varying water column depths. Strommel was able to streamline his mathematical calculations. However, with no Coriolis Effect in place, 80 million cubic meters of water in the box simply went around and around.

Realizing that he had miscalculated, Strommel added a varying Coriolis effect and this forced the hill of water next to the Florida coastline. It also showed that the flow is in an elliptical, rather than a circular form.

The bottom line on ocean movement: the ocean is in motion anytime that you have a pressure gradient.

Vorticity is also highly connected with ocean motion. It affects which way the current is going to flow.

Cold core eddies: Rotate counterclockwise.
Warm core eddies: Rotate clockwise.
Rotation is reversed in the Southern Hemisphere.

Locating the warm and cold water eddies is simple:

South side of the Gulf Stream = Cold core eddy.
North side of the Gulf Stream = Warm core eddy.

In the world's oceans, thermohaline circulation is coupled with and driven by surface water circulation, as shown in the diagram below:

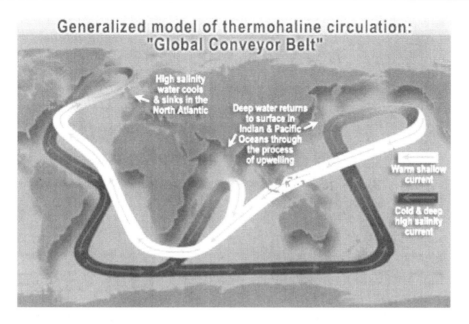

The term **thermohaline** refers to temperature "thermo" and salinity "haline," the two factors that drive this circulation pattern. As warmer surface water, known as the Gulf Stream, travels up the coast of eastern North America, it eventually meets cold dry air from Canada. This continental air cools and evaporates some of the surface water, leaving it colder and more saline than before. The formation of polar ice also removes more freshwater, making the ocean water even saltier. This dense, cold ocean water sinks and travels back down along the east side of the North American continent, driving the overall circulation patterns.

Patterns of deep ocean circulation are affected in part by the shapes of the continents, by the need to maintain a water balance in different parts of the ocean, and by areas of upwelling. Surface water sinks down into the deep ocean at the top of the Gulf Stream, and then travels away from that area along North and South America, and subsequently along Antarctica. Deep waters return to the surface in areas of upwelling; these occur in the Indian Ocean, in the North Pacific offshore of Oregon, and in the South Pacific offshore of Peru and Chile. Areas of upwelling are very rich in nutrients and are excellent fisheries resources. Water requires approximately 1000 years to travel along the entire circulation pattern.

Thermohaline circulation is very important in regulating climate and vice versa. Global warming can slow down thermohaline circulation through the melting of sea ice and glaciers at the poles. When large amounts of freshwater are added at the poles, it counteracts the evaporation that normally occurs and seawater does not sink, because it does not become more saline or denser. It has been hypothesized (and there is evidence in the geologic record) that this could stop global thermohaline circulation altogether.

Thermohaline circulation strongly affects the climate of the continents through the movement of warm surface waters. For example, if this circulation were to stop, the Gulf Stream would not travel up the eastern United States and across to the United Kingdom, and it would be much colder in these areas than it is now. The ultimate effects of such changes are difficult to fully predict, but it is certain they would have significant impacts on local climate, agriculture, and fisheries resources.

Skill 8.6   Identify the effects of human activity on the coastal and marine environment.

One of the most significant effects of human activity on the coastline is the building of **structures** that affect coastal morphology. In many areas, sand would normally be transported along a beach due to wave action, and beaches and sandbars would shift with time and major weather events. However, homeowners and businesses frequently build in these areas, as they are desirable locations. This creates a need to control and retain the beach. It is becoming increasingly clear that it is difficult or impossible to do so over the long-term. The photo below shows how jetties and groins retain sand behind them, but deplete sand in areas beyond. A jetty that protects one person's beach may destroy another further along.

Seawalls and **riprap** placed along shorelines are intended to protect property from erosion, but reflect wave energy back. This increased wave energy increases erosion of beaches in front of the seawall and may eventually cause undermining of the structure. Properties with riprap in front of them may one day lose their beach entirely, as shown in the photo below:

Another way that shorelines are altered is the through the **filling of wetlands** and the **channelization** of major rivers. These alterations reduce the ability of shoreline areas to absorb flooding, tidal surges, and temporary sea surges from adverse weather events like hurricanes. They also change the shape of river deltas and reduce the formation of natural barrier islands, which are also protective and highly biologically productive. **Dredging** and channelization of major rivers may reduce the amount of nutrient-rich sediment that is available for deposit in coastal areas, reducing its productivity.

Pollution from human activities eventually makes its way to the sea, where it has a variety of impacts. Sewage discharges may result in algal blooms and dead zones associated with excessive nutrients and oxygen demand. This type of discharge may also kill coral reefs, destroying highly productive marine habitat. Contaminants in discharges may cause sediments to be unfit for small sediment-dwelling organisms, which form the basis of the food chain for fish and birds. Shellfish, fish, wildlife, and seabirds may become contaminated and experience toxic effects, or become unfit for human consumption.

Global climate change is also projected to have several detrimental effects on coastlines and ocean resources. Sea level rise is expected to occur, flooding coastal areas, including major cities around the world in which 60% of Earth's population resides. A rise in the ocean's surface temperature may intensify storms and monsoon seasons, increasing flooding and damage to coastal structures. A change in ocean circulation patterns with increased warming has also been hypothesized and observed in the geologic record. This would have dramatic effects on the climate in coastal regions, as well as fisheries.

An increase in CO_2 absorption by the oceans helps offset warming, but also acidifies the oceans. This effect is being observed, and has the potential to dissolve the shells of many tiny creatures that serve as the base of the food chain. Coral reefs are suffering from bleaching from increased surface ocean temperatures, and will be adversely affected by acidification.

The melting of polar sea ice will have a variety of effects, including dramatic changes to habitat of polar bears, penguins, and other polar species and the human communities that rely on them. Among the few positive effects of global warming, the absence of polar sea ice is also expected to benefit oil, natural gas, and mineral exploration and open up new sea-lanes for world trade.

Overfishing is having significant impacts on the world's fisheries and food supplies, as well as marine mammals and seabirds that depend on fish. Many fishing methods are still employed that are highly destructive, including bottom trawls, which churn up and destroy the seabed, and blasting or cyanide poisoning of coral reefs. **Fish farming** is another destructive practice that provides fish or shellfish for certain populations, while introducing fish waste and antibiotics into the environment. This may introduce weaker genetic strains and diseases into wild populations. Natural habitats such as mangroves are often destroyed to create these areas, and ground up wild fish are frequently used as feed—often destroying more wild fish, pound for pound, than the food species being raised.

COMPETENCY 9.0   KNOWLEDGE OF THE FACTORS THAT INFLUENCE AMTOSPHERIC CONDITIONS AND WEATHER

Skill 9.1   **Analyze the composition and structure of the atmosphere and how it protects life and insulates the planet.**

The Atmosphere

Earth's atmosphere is very similar to a fluid. The atmosphere makes up only 0.25% of what we call Earth, and like the fluids of the ocean, our atmosphere is driven by heat, primarily solar radiation. Having an atmosphere is not unique for a planet. To a degree, most of the planets in our solar system have an atmosphere; however, the presence of significant oxygen in Earth's atmosphere is unique and makes life possible on our planet. Earth's atmosphere is composed of 78% nitrogen, 21% oxygen, and 1% other gasses.

Components of the Atmosphere

Water vapor: Along with carbon dioxide (CO_2) and methane, water vapor (H_2O) is considered a **greenhouse gas**: a gas that absorbs heat energy. Water vapor is the most prevalent of the greenhouse gasses and is especially good at collecting heat energy, as evidenced by Earth's ability to retain heat at night when solar radiation is lowest.

Dust and aerosols: These are natural components of the atmosphere and their presence produces optical phenomena such as making the sky appear blue, rainbows, and the Northern and Southern Lights.

Pollutants: Some are man-made, including industrial waste, chemical refrigerants and hydrocarbons released from burning fossil fuels. Some are natural such as Terpene leased from trees, Saharan dust, and CO_2 released by volcanoes.

Layers of the Atmosphere

Troposphere: (Ground level to 11Km, 0 to 17.6 miles, or 0 to 92,928 feet.) The troposphere varies in height according to the temperature. It is lower at the poles and higher at the equator. Because the pressure decreases, it gets colder as you go up in the troposphere. Only very rarely do you have a mixing between the troposphere and the next layer, the stratosphere. All storms, weather fronts, and weather occur in the troposphere.

Stratosphere: (11Km to 50Km, 17.6 to 80 miles, or 92,980 to 422,400 feet.) The stratosphere is characterized by weak vertical air motion, and strong horizontal air motion. There is very little lifting or sinking air in the stratosphere.

Temperatures warm as you go up due to the presence of the ozone layer contained within the stratosphere.

Mesosphere: (50 to 85Km, 80 to 136 miles, or 422,400 to 718,080 feet.) It is bitterly cold in the mesosphere.

Thermosphere: (85 to 600Km, 136 to 960 miles, or 718,000 to 5,068,800 feet.) This is the hottest portion of the atmosphere with rapid warming accompanying a rise in altitude. There are very few molecules left to block out the incoming solar radiation. The outer reaches of the thermosphere are also sometimes referred to as the exosphere.

Ionosphere: (Located within the upper portion of the mesosphere at 80Km and goes into the thermosphere). The ionosphere is an area of **free ions**: positively charged ions, produced as a result of solar radiation striking the atmosphere. The solar wind strikes the Ionosphere at the polar dips in the magnetosphere. The ions are excited to a higher energy state and this energy is released into the visible spectrum to form the **Aurora Borealis** (Northern Lights).

Ozone layer (O_3) (contained within the stratosphere): Ozone is essential to life on Earth and is continually formed and destroyed within the atmosphere. Only a very thin layer of ozone protects against UV (ultra violet) radiation. Ultra violet radiation scrambles the DNA codes in human cells, and can kill the cells or, at a minimum, cause cancer.

There is much concern about a hole in the ozone layer. This is a misnomer. In reality, there is not a hole, but a possible thinning of the layer. Many scientists believe this is due to the presence of CFC's (Carbon Fluorocarbons). The chlorine (Cl) in CFCs and from other sources steals an oxygen atom from Ozone (O_3) molecules. This theft leaves behind only plain oxygen (O_2), which does not effectively screen out UV radiation. $Cl + O_3 = ClO + O_2$. However, the resultant ClO molecule is very unstable and UV radiation can easily break it apart. The released chlorine then attacks another ozone molecule and the process repeats itself.

CFCs were thought to be the primary culprit, but this theory has problems. CFCs were only invented in the 1920's for use in aerosol spray cans, industrial processes, and refrigerants. Although it may be a contributor in the depletion of the ozone layer, not all scientists believe the theory that CFC's are solely responsible. Why does the thinning occur over only the Antarctica? The greatest use of CFCs occurred in the industrialized nations of the Northern Hemisphere. Additionally, the hole varies in size from year to year, appearing during the Antarctic spring in October and disappearing by mid November or December. There is a lack of data. Data related to this thinning has only been collected since 1979. There is a possibility that the hole may have been there before the introduction of CFCs. An alternate theory to CFCs is **Circumpolar Vortex**.

Because there is a great deal of open ocean at Antarctica, it is a very cold place during the winter. The cold, in effect, isolates the Antarctic atmosphere from the rest of the warmer atmosphere. This extreme cold forms ice crystals in the atmosphere and chlorine (Cl) is locked into the crystals. When the Antarctic spring comes, the atmosphere thaws out, releasing the chlorine into the atmosphere. The chlorine attacks the ozone layer, decreasing its density. As spring progresses, the circumpolar vortex weakens, allowing the air to mix with the normally ozone rich air. Thus, the hole disappears.

Skill 9.2 **Differentiate between the sources, characteristics, and movement of air masses (e.g., maritime, continental, polar, tropical).**

Air masses are large bodies of air that have a similar temperature, atmospheric pressure, and moisture content. The characteristics of the world's air masses are largely determined by where they are formed, as shown in the chart below:

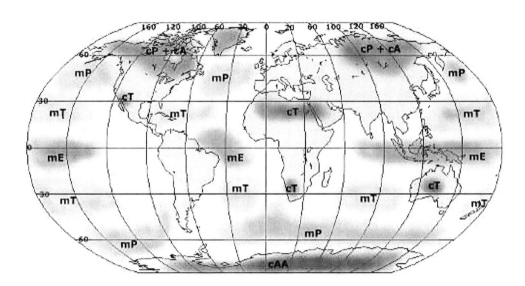

Warmer air masses are formed near the tropics ("T"), both over the ocean (maritime "m"), and over the continents ("c"). Cold air masses are formed in polar regions (polar "p" and Arctic or Antarctic "A"). Dryer air masses are formed over continents, while moisture-laden air masses are formed over the ocean. As an air mass moves, it may gain moisture if it moves over the water, or lose moisture as it moves over land.

As with ocean currents, warm air masses will tend to move toward the poles, losing heat as they go. Cold, polar air masses will move down toward the equator. Because of Coriolis forces, air masses move in a circular manner, and also circulate upward from Earth and back down again, in cells as shown below.

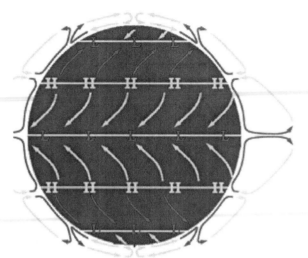

Areas where hot air masses are rising away from Earth create low-pressure zones, and areas where cold air masses are sinking down create high-pressure zones. Surface air masses generally move toward latitudes of low pressure and away from latitudes of high pressure. These latitudes of high and low pressure are known as **pressure belts**.

Locally, the movement of air masses may also be affected by continental landforms, such as mountains.

Skill 9.3   Identify characteristics of high and low pressure systems, including the formation of fronts and severe weather systems.

High and Low Pressure Areas

Surface pressure is affected by temperature and reflects what is happening in the the air. This is very useful for predicting changes in the weather. Temperature plays a large part in the changes in upper atmosphere air pressure.

Pressure is the force exerted by the molecules in the air. If you take two columns of air (A & B), with the same temperature and same density, and raise the temperature of B and lower the temperature of A, then you will cause an expansion or contraction of the columns of air.

- Column A contracts because you are lowering the temperature. The molecules become less energetic and are packed closer together, hence, denser.

- Column B expands because you've raised the temperature. The molecules become more active and are packed more loosely, hence, less dense.

- Although the columns now are of physically differing sizes (volume), the pressure is identical in both columns because the density has adjusted for the difference in volume.

- However, the atmosphere is not neatly isolated into columns. So another way to consider this pressure change is to visualize two columns of air not isolated from each other.

- Columns A and B both have the same temperature, density, and pressure throughout. Now cool the air in column A and heat the air in column B. Overlay these two columns of air with a scale calibrated in millibars. The air in column B now has a higher pressure than the air in column A when both are at the same altitude.

Meterogically, the air in column A represents an area of **low pressure**, and the air in column B represents an area of **high pressure**. Since nature abhors a vacuum, the air tries to move from the area of high pressure to the area of low pressure. Surface pressure in column A starts to rise because the air is moving in. Surface pressure in column B starts to drop because the air is moving out.

For use in weather prediction, the effect of temperature is more important to changes in upper atmosphere air pressure than to changes in the surface pressure. Temperature has the biggest effect on air pressure in the atmosphere.

Weather maps reflect areas of high and low pressure. In general, the undulating surface is lower to the North and higher to the South. However, the surface has waves in it forming troughs and ridges. These correspond to troughs of low pressure and ridges of high pressure. Surface lows are always offset to the right.

Front: a narrow zone of transition between air masses of different densities that is usually due to temperature contrasts. Because they are associated with temperature, fronts are usually referred to as either warm or cold.

Warm front: a front whose movement causes the warm air (less dense) to advance, while the cold air (more dense) retreats. A warm front usually triggers a cloud development sequence of cirrus, cirrostratus, altostratus, nimbostratus and stratus clouds. It may result in an onset of light rain or snowfall immediately ahead of the front, which gives way as the cloud sequence forms, to steady precipitation (light to moderate), until the front passes, a time frame that may exceed 24 hours.

The gentle rains associated with a warm front are normally welcomed by farmers. However, if it is cold enough for snow to fall, the snow may significantly accumulate. If the air is unstable, cumulonimbus clouds may develop, and brief, intense thunderstorms may punctuate the otherwise gentler rain or snowfall.

Cold front: a front whose movement causes the cold air (more dense) to displace the warm air (less dense). The results of cold front situations depend on the stability of the air. If the air is stable, nimbostratus and altostratus clouds may form, and brief showers may immediately precede the front.

If the air is unstable, there is greater uplift, cumulonimbus clouds may tower over nimbostratus clouds, and cirrus clouds are blown downstream from the cumulonimbus by the winds at high altitude. Thunderstorms may occur, accompanied by gusty surface winds and hail, as well as other, more violent weather. If the cold front moves quickly (roughly 28 mph or greater), a squall line of thunderstorms may form either right ahead of the front or up to 180 miles ahead of it.

Occluded front: a front where a cold front has caught up to a warm front and has intermingled, usually by sliding under the warmer air. Cold fronts generally move faster than warm fronts and occasionally overrun slower moving warm fronts. The weather ahead of an occluded front is similar to that of a warm front during its advance, but switches to that of a cold front as the cold front passes through.

Stationary front: a front that shows no overall movement. The weather produced by this front can vary widely and depends on the amount of moisture present and the relative motions of the air pockets along the front. Most of the precipitation falls on the cold side of the front.

Tornado: an area of extreme low pressure, with rapidly rotating winds beneath a cumulonimbus cloud. Tornadoes are normally spawned from a supercell thunderstorm. They can occur when very cold air and very warm air meet, usually in the spring.

Tornadoes represent the lowest pressure points on Earth and move across the landscape at an average speed of 30 mph. The average size of a tornado is 100 yards, but they can be as large a mile wide. A tornado's wind speed ranges from 65 to 300 mph and has an average duration of 10 to 15 minutes, but has been known to last up to 3 hours. Tornadoes usually occur in the late afternoon (3 to 7 p.m.) in conjunction with the rear of a thunderstorm. Most tornadoes spin counter-clockwise in the northern hemisphere, and spin clockwise in the southern hemisphere.

Worldwide, the U.S. has the most tornadoes and most of these occur in the spring. Texas has the most tornadoes, but Florida has the largest number per square mile. Tornadoes are without a doubt the most violent of all storms. Roughly 120 people each year are killed in the United States by tornadoes.

Formation of a Tornado

Technically, tornadoes are actually classified as mesocyclones that form within super cell thunderstorms. Temperature differentials within the thunderstorm cause an up and down draft effect that induces a horizontal spinning motion. An increase in the up and down motion tightens the spin and a strong draft may eventually tilt the **mesocyclone** into a vertical position. When this occurs, the bottom of the cloud wall drops down as a funnel cloud. If the funnel cloud touches the ground, it becomes a tornado. Approximately 50% of mesocyclones produce tornadoes.

Tornadoes are very rare in **pop-up** and **squall line thunderstorms**. These are both isolated storm fronts of very short duration and speeds. Although there is an induced spin similar to a mesocyclone, it is on a much smaller scale. Tornadoes sometimes form **families**: multiple funnels within the same super cell thunderstorm. If all of these funnels touch the ground, a very rare tornado formation known as a **rake** can, as the name implies, affect a much wider area in its path.

Hurricanes

Hurricanes are produced by temperature and pressure differentials between the tropical seas and the atmosphere.

Powered by heat from the sea, they are steered by the easterly trade winds and the temperate westerlies, as well as their own incredible energy. Hurricane development starts in June in the Atlantic, Caribbean, and Gulf of Mexico, and lasts until the end of hurricane season in late November.

Hurricanes are called by different names depending on their location. In the Indian Ocean they are called **cyclones**. In the Atlantic, and east of the international dateline in the Pacific, they are called Hurricanes. In the western Pacific they are called **typhoons**. Regardless of the name, a hurricane can be up to 500 miles across, last for over two weeks from inception to death, and can produce devastation on an immense scale.

Formation of a Hurricane

Hurricanes start as an upper atmospheric disturbance at the 500mb altitude. This is a trough of low pressure called a **tropical wave**.

Recipe for a hurricane:
Warm water at least 200 feet in depth and 79° F temperature.
Converging surface winds.
Diverging upper atmosphere winds, diverging at a faster rate than the surface winds are converging.

High humidity and unstable air (warm air rising).
Moderate strength winds aloft, and they must blow from the same direction to add momentum to the self-propagating effect.

Warm water feeds hurricanes. The greater the mass of water available, the greater the spin induced by the winds going in the same direction. The storm essentially rotates counter- clockwise around itself, pulling in more wind in a self-perpetuating effect.

Divergence causes the storm to grow as the condensation of the cloud mass releases heat to further feed the storm. Bands of clear air form between the spiral bands (thunderstorms) of the hurricane and a clear, low-pressure **eye** forms at the center of the storm.

The tightness of the eye indicates the relative strength of the storm. The more pronounced and tight the eye is, the stronger the storm. The highest winds are located next to the eye wall. Although, as a general rule, hurricanes move east to west, a hurricane's path is determined by its interaction with areas of high and low-pressure cells. These cells steer the storm with lows repelling it and highs attracting it.

Hurricanes die when they move over land or cold water. The hurricane's energy dissipates slowly when robbed of its water or heat source. Stable air breaks the self-propagating effect.

Skill 9.4   Identify factors that cause local winds (i.e., land and sea breezes) and global winds (e.g., pressure belts, Coriolis effect)

Small Scale Wind Systems

Small-scale wind systems are found in the area of surface winds (<I,000 m altitude), and are affected by surface friction caused by the topography.

Turbulence is caused by surface heating and the effect of topography on the wind's movement. An increase in surface heating creates greater turbulence.

Eddies are formed when surface winds hit an obstruction. This causes an air pocket to form that diminishes or changes the direction of the wind trapped in the eddy. Pilots refer to eddies as **windshear**.

Waves are formed as the result of wind moving across a body of water.

Wind direction refers to the direction from which the wind is blowing.

Prevailing Winds is the term used to describe the dominant direction from which the wind is blowing.

Sea breezes are caused by the temperature differentials between the land and oceans. During the day, the land is hot and the water is cool, and wind blows from the sea to the land.

Land breezes follow the reverse pattern of sea breezes, with evening cooling of the land causing airflow from the land to the sea.

Monsoons are seasonal land and sea breezes that are characterized by extreme rains during the summer and dry winters. Monsoons are found almost exclusively in tropical zones because the temperature differentials are greatest in those areas.

Mountain and Valley breezes are the result of thermal differences and topography. During the day the thermal currents rise up from the valley floor and move up the sides of the mountains. At night, the mountains act as a lingering heat source, retaining the heat in the valleys.

A **Chinook breeze** occurs when the prevailing westerlies are squeezed between the bottom of the Stratosphere and the top of large mountain ranges. This causes heating and expansion of the air as it moves over the mountains, drying the area and melting snow. This effect can be intensified by the presence of high and low pressure systems. Example: The Chinook Breeze is most heavily concentrated on the eastern edge of the Rocky Mountains. Its presence can cause an early melt of the snow, increasing the likelihood of flooding downstream.

Santa Ana Winds are a specialized form of Chinook Breeze. They are formed when air moves down the valleys to the coast when a high-pressure area is present. The wind is very warm and dry, creating dangerous fire conditions.

A **haboob** is seen in the deserts and is a dynamic of thunderstorms that do not have enough condensation to precipitate. It is characterized by violent up and down drafts that pick up sand and carry it far up into the atmosphere. This sand rains down thousands of miles away.

Urban heat islands are the result of concentrated masses of buildings and concrete and asphalt paving. The heat produced by activities in the urban areas and then re-radiated by the concrete forms a rising thermal zone over the urban area. This is why it is usually 10 degrees or more hotter in the city than the countryside. The concrete buildings and asphalt paving absorbs more heat than grass and fields in the countryside.

Lake effect snow/rain is caused by air moving over a large body of water. The air absorbs large amounts of moisture and then releases it as snow or rain (dependent on temperature) over urban heat islands. Example: Situated close to the large lakes, Chicago, Illinois, and Buffalo, New York often experience unexpected precipitation or early snowfall during the fall months because of the lake effect. This usually ceases when the lakes freeze over during the winter months.

Pressure belts are important in determining the movement of global air masses and winds, and are introduced and diagrammed in Skill 10.2. Low pressure belts occur at the equator and at polar latitudes (approximately 60° N and S) and high pressure belts occur at mid-latitudes (approximately 30° N and S).

The **Coriolis effect** is the deflection of air or water currents caused by the rotation of Earth. This creates global wind patterns that affect the climate. These wind patterns also represent rain patterns. The wind patterns between 30°N and 0°N, are called the **trade winds**. The wind patterns between 30°N and 60°N are called the **prevailing westerlies**. All the great deserts of the world lie between the Tropics at 0° and 30°North and South latitudes. A shift in the wind patterns would also shift the deserts. The optimum growing zone is between 30° and 60° North and South latitudes.

Global Wind Patterns

The rise and fall of heat at the 0°, 30°, 60°, and 90' latitudes drive convection cells by causing the pressure gradients to speed up or slow down. **Jet streams** are zones of very strong, moving air confined to narrow columns and they mark the zones where the cold polar air and the warmer air meet. This produces the greatest pressure gradients. Jet streams can be either straight or dramatically dip, creating ridges and troughs on the 500-300mb pressure surface.

The flatter the isobars, the more evenly balanced the weather. The more pronounced the ridges and troughs, the more pronounced the swings in the weather.

The ITCZ (**Inter Tropical Convergence Zone**) controls the weather in the tropics, and it moves north and south of the equator. The ITCZ is responsible for the formation of Monsoon rains.

The **horse latitudes** are located between 0° and 30° north and south latitudes. While the **doldrums**, an area of no wind, is located at 0°.

The **trade winds** are very strong and blow all the time in the horse latitudes. The trade winds also provide direct heating to the coastal climate in this zone.

The **prevailing westerlies** are found between 30° and 60° north and south latitude. These cause storms and winds to move in a west to east pattern.

Polar winds are the product of the presence or absence of sunlight, not polar cells.

Skill 9.5 Determine how the transfer of energy throughout the atmosphere influences weather conditions (e.g., hydrologic cycle).

(See Skill 4.4 for a discussion of the hydrologic cycle and Skill 9.3 for a discussion of fronts and weather conditions.)

Weather occurs as a result of heat transfer in the atmosphere. The source of this heat is the Sun, and this energy reaches Earth via radiation. The air just above Earth's surface is in turn heated by conduction, as the air touches the Sun-warmed surface. As heated air expands and rises, it sets up convection currents, which are another way heat energy is transferred. The movement of air in the atmosphere is complex, but in general, warm air moves toward the poles and cooler air flows toward the equator. This creates a pattern of atmospheric circulation that leads to areas of sinking air and rising air. High pressure systems are found in areas of sinking air, while low pressure systems are found in areas of rising air. The movements of air in the atmosphere are responsible for the generation and distribution of weather patterns.

Skill 9.6 Interpret weather maps and the indicated atmospheric conditions.

Once you can read a station plot you can begin to perform map analyses. Meteorologists use station plots to draw lines of constant pressure (isobars), temperature (isotherms), and dewpoint (isodrosotherms) to achieve an understanding of the current state of the atmosphere. This knowledge ultimately leads to better weather forecasts and warnings. Decoding these plots is easier than it may seem. The values are located in a form similar to a tic-tac-toe pattern.

In the upper left, the temperature is plotted in Fahrenheit. In this example, the temperature is 77°F.

Along the center, the cloud types are indicated. The top symbol is the high-level cloud type followed by the mid-level cloud type. The lowest symbol represents low-level cloud over a number that indicates the height of the base of that cloud (in hundreds of feet). In this example, the high level cloud is cirrus, the mid-level cloud is altocumulus and the low-level cloud is a cumulonimbus with a base height of 2000 feet.

At the upper right is the atmospheric pressure reduced to mean sea level in millibars (mb) to the nearest tenth with the leading 9 or 10 omitted. In this case the pressure would be 999.8 mb. If the pressure was plotted as 024 it would be 1002.4 mb. When trying to determine whether to add a 9 or 10 use the number that will give you a value closest to 1000 mb.

On the second row, the number on the far left is the visibility in miles. In this example, the visibility is 5 miles.

Next to the visibility is the present weather symbol. There are 95 symbols which represent the weather that is either presently occurring or has ended within the previous hour. In this example, a light rain shower was occurring at the time of the observation.

The circle symbol in the center represents the amount of total cloud cover reported in eighths. This cloud cover includes all low, middle, and high level clouds. In this example, 7/8th of the sky was covered with clouds.

This number and symbol tell how much the pressure has changed (in tenths of millibars) in the past three hours and the trend in the change of the pressure during that same period. In this example, the pressure was steady and then fell (lowered) becoming 0.3 millibars LOWER than it was three hours ago.

These lines indicate wind direction and speed rounded to the nearest 5 knots. The longest line, extending from the sky cover plot, points in the direction that the wind is blowing **from**. Thus, in this case, the wind is blowing **from** the southwest. The shorter lines, called barbs, indicate the wind speed in knots (kt). The speed of the wind is calculated by the barbs. Each long barb represents 10 kt with short barbs representing 5 kt. In this example, the station plot contains two long barbs so the wind speed is 20 kt, or about 24 mph.

The 71 at the lower left is the dewpoint temperature. The dewpoint temperature is the temperature the air would have to cool to become saturated, or in other words reach a relative humidity of 100%.

The lower right area is reserved for the past weather, which is the most significant weather that has occurred within the past six hours excluding the most recent hour.

Analyze a Map on Your Own

The following are a few sources of current weather maps. Sometimes a site may be down or experiencing data losses. In such a case, try another site listed. This is not meant to be an exhaustive list. These are provided for your convenience.

- NCAR, pick your regional plot: http://www.rap.ucar.edu/weather/surface/
- UNISYS: http://weather.unisys.com/surface/sfc_map.html
- College of DuPage: http://weather.cod.edu/analysis/analysis.sfcplots.html
- NOAA http://www.nws.noaa.gov/
- Ohio State University: http://asp1.sbs.ohio-state.edu/ (Click on "Surface Wx" and choose "Current Analysis.")

Weather Map Symbols

Surface Station Model

Temp (F) Weather Dewpoint (F)		Pressure (mb) Sky Cover Wind (kts)	**Data at Surface Station** Temp 45 °F, dewpoint 29 °F, overcast, wind **from** SE at 15 knots, weather light rain, pressure 1004.5 mb

Upper Air Station Model

Temp (C) Dewpoint (C)		Height (m) Wind (kts)	**Data at Pressure Level - 850 mb** Temp -5 °C, dewpoint -12 °C, wind **from** S at 75 knots, height of level 1564 m

Forecast Station Model

Temp (F) Weather Dewpoint (F)		PoP (%) Sky Cover Wind (kts)	**Forecast at Valid Time** Temp 78 °F, dewpoint 64 °F, scattered clouds, wind **from** E at 10 knots, probability of precipitation 70% with rain showers

Map Symbols

Sky Cover	Wind
○ clear	◎ Calm
◐ 1/8	___ 1-2 knots (1-2 mph)
◕ scattered	___ 3-7 knots (3-8 mph)
◑ 3/8	___ 8-12 knots (9-14 mph)
◖ 4/8	___ 13-17 knots (15-20 mph)
◕ 5/8	___ 18-22 knots (21-25 mph)
◕ broken	___ 23-27 knots (26-31 mph)
◕ 7/8	___ 48-52 knots (55-60 mph)
● overcast	___ 73-77 knots (84-89 mph)
⊗ obscured	___ 103-107 knots (119-123 mph)
⊕ missing	Shaft in direction wind is coming **from**

Skill 9.7 **Evaluate how local weather is affected by geographic features (e.g., proximity to bodies of water, urban versus rural settings, unequal heating of land and water).**

Mountains are one of the primary geographic features that affect the weather. As moisture-laden, relatively cool air comes in off the ocean, it is forced to rise when it meets a mountain range. As it rises, it cools until the dew point is reached (when it can no longer hold the water it is carrying). The water precipitates out as rain or snow and falls in the foothills and in the mountains. As the air mass crosses the mountains and goes down the other side, it sinks and is warmed by the landmass. This air mass has already lost moisture, and it is able to absorb more moisture as it warms up, creating a very dry area beyond the mountains (called a rain shadow). Inland deserts can frequently be found just past mountain ranges (for example, on the western coast of North America).

The different atmospheric conditions between the mountains and the valley or desert areas can also result in winds. Winds are generally caused by differences in heat and pressure gradients. Air masses that pass from continental interiors over mountain ranges may be rapidly heated as they descend and result in hot dry winds along coastlines, such as the Santa Ana winds of California, the Mistral of France, or the Chinook of the Pacific Northwest and western Canada. Colder katabatic winds can be formed by differential heating of mountaintops compared to valleys, and result in a colder wind blowing down from the mountains.

Even small differences in **elevation,** caused by hills or depressions, can affect the weather. Higher elevations are generally colder, and lower elevations are generally hotter. Higher elevations that experience freezing temperatures, or where air masses are forced to heights where the air temperature is freezing, will experience snow, sleet, or hail more often than lower elevations.

Urban versus rural settings can have an effect on local weather conditions as well. Urban areas tend to trap heat, as well as generate their own. This leads to densely populated/built-up areas being hotter than surrounding rural areas—an effect known as "urban heat island." This excess heat in urban areas can even lead to an increase in thunderstorms locally.

A lack of vegetation and permeable ground partially contributes to the urban heat island effect. Trees provide shade, as well as increase evapotranspiration, both of which help to cool an area. Emissions from cars and industry can lead to the formation of clouds and smog, both of which help trap heat. Also, our cities' structures tend to lose heat very slowly, meaning that the heat island effect is more pronounced at night. Long after rural areas have cooled down for the night, city streets and buildings are still radiating the heat of the day.

Proximity to large bodies of water also affects the weather in an area. Ocean temperatures are very stable when compared to continental temperatures, and tend to have moderate temperature extremes. Thus, coastal areas will have milder summers and winters than inland areas. Very **large lakes**, such as the Great Lakes, can have a similar effect. Coastal areas, and areas near very large lakes and rivers, also tend to have more humidity and more rain and snow than inland areas.

Another aspect of weather along coastlines is **wind,** caused by the unequal heating of land and water. Along the coast, the ocean stays at roughly the same temperature most of the time. However, the land heats up during the day and cools at night. During the day, air flows from the cool ocean to the warm land, creating an onshore breeze. If the land cools at night to temperatures lower than the ocean, a breeze may form going offshore. Coastal areas near the equator are especially prone to sea breezes. Florida experiences coastal breezes from both the Atlantic Ocean and the Gulf of Mexico, often at the same time. These "breezes" can collide in the center of the state and create spectacular thunder, lightning, and hailstorms.

Skill 9.8   Identify characteristics of weather systems that affect Florida.

Typical Weather

Florida is influenced by warm subtropical Gulf Stream and Gulf of Mexico waters, and maintains a relatively even temperature throughout the year, ranging from 60° F in the winter to 90° F in the summer. Like most of the Caribbean, Florida enjoys clear, sunny weather a very large percentage of the time, with frequent light afternoon rain showers. Because it is surrounded by water on three sides, and has numerous lakes, rivers, canals, and wetlands, the humidity is relatively high. Similar to many subtropical areas, central and south Florida have a wet warm season from June–October, and a dry cool season from November–May.

Like many coastal areas, Florida experiences an afternoon sea breeze caused by differential warming between land and sea. Sea breezes converge in central Florida from both sides–the Gulf of Mexico and the Atlantic. Where they meet, thunderstorms frequently occur due to temperature imbalances in the converging winds. These can form very quickly and normally last no more than 30 minutes, but may present hazards related to lightning strikes, high winds, flash floods, and tornadoes. Tornadoes may arise from the most severe thunderstorms, and are most frequent in the spring and summer.

Tropical Storms and Hurricanes

During the summer and fall (June-November), Florida may experience tropical storms and hurricanes that form in the Atlantic Ocean. In general, ocean temperature must be at least 80° at the surface with a high humidity for a hurricane to form. As the surface of the ocean warms up in the summer, hot air rises and cooler air rushes in to take its place. Thunderstorms at sea produce the initial winds that eventually turn into hurricanes, just as they are responsible for tornadoes on land. Due to Coriolis forces, a circular pattern of very high-velocity wind occurs (up to 200 miles/hr). As the hot air rises, it eventually cools and produces a heavy rain, which adds to the destructive force of the hurricane. Hurricane winds at the surface of the ocean create storm surges that can be as high as 30-40 feet. These surges cause flooding and damage when the hurricane reaches land.

Hurricanes in the Atlantic Ocean generally form to the west of Africa and are carried to southeast North America by prevailing ocean winds. There, the local wind patterns may cause them to impact the Caribbean Islands, the northeast coast of Mexico, Florida, states located in the Gulf of Mexico, or southern states along the Atlantic coast. Rarely, a hurricane will proceed farther inland or up the Atlantic coast as far as Massachusetts.

Hurricane Damage

The destruction and damage caused by a hurricane or tropical storm can be severe. **Storm surge** causes most of the damage as the winds push along a wall of rising water in their path, and this rising effect is amplified on low sloping shorelines such as found on the Gulf Coast. The intense winds can also cause damage. Some notable storms:

Florida Keys, 1935: A category 5 hurricane, the biggest of the 20th century, was recorded having 150-200 mph winds and a barometric pressure of 892 mb.

Hurricane Camille, Florida and South Carolina, 1969: This category 5 hurricane with a barometric pressure of 990 mb, scored a direct hit on the Gulf Coast, killing 300 people and causing severe flooding as far north as Virginia.

Hurricane Andrew, Gulf Coast, 1992: Classified as a category 4/5 hurricane, this is the fastest moving storm ever recorded. Moving at 20 mph, the hurricane had maximum sustained winds of 150 mph and gusts up to 175 mph, and re-intensified just prior to making landfall. Andrew was a notable exception to the damage rule in that it was the winds, not the storm surge (16.9 feet), which caused the majority of the 26.5 billion dollars of damage. Over 80,000 houses were destroyed and an additional 50,000 houses suffered greater than 50% damage. 70,000 acres of mangrove swamp was uprooted as this storm cut a 25 mile wide path of destruction in Florida and Louisiana.

Global Effects

El Niño and La Niña events greatly affect Florida's weather patterns. El Niño years are warmer and wetter than usual, and the Jet Stream stays further south, driving more storms across Florida in the winter. The resulting precipitation recharges groundwater aquifers and provides relief from drought, but can also cause flooding if it occurs after a year of high rainfall. La Niña events result in colder and dryer weather than usual, and can be associated with droughts.

Skill 9.9   Evaluate how global climate influences, such as jet streams and ocean currents, affect weather (e.g., El Niño).

(For a discussion of jet streams and El Niño see Skill 10.4.)

World weather patterns are greatly influenced by ocean surface currents in the upper layer of the ocean. These currents continuously move along the ocean surface in specific directions. Ocean currents that flow deep below the surface are called sub-surface currents. These currents are influenced by such factors as the location of landmasses in the current's path and Earth's rotation.

Surface currents are caused by winds and are classified by temperature. Cold currents originate in the polar regions and flow through surrounding water that is measurably warmer. Those currents with a higher temperature than the surrounding water are called warm currents and can be found near the equator. These currents follow swirling routes around the ocean basins and the equator. Warm currents bring warm air with them; cold currents tend to make the air above them cooler.

The Gulf Stream and the California Current are the two main surface currents that flow along the coastlines of the United States. The Gulf Stream is a warm current in the Atlantic Ocean that carries warm water from the equator to the northern parts of the Atlantic Ocean. The Gulf Stream brings warmth to northwestern Europe, resulting in temperatures significantly above average for that latitude. The California Current has the opposite effect of the Gulf Stream. It is a cold current that originates in the Arctic regions and flows southward along the west coast of the United States.

COMPETENCY 10.0   KNOWLEDGE OF EARTH'S CLIMATE PATTERNS

Skill 10.1   Identify the factors that contribute to the climate of a geographic area.

Many factors affect an area's climate, including latitude, elevation and relief, ocean currents, direction of prevailing winds, and distance from the sea.

An area's **latitude** plays a role in determining how warm or cool the area is. For example, the equator receives more direct sunlight than anywhere else on Earth, year round. Therefore, low-latitude regions are warmer than high latitude regions.

The **elevation** and **relief** of a given region affect the climate in a few ways. Firstly, higher regions tend to be cooler than low-lying areas because air temperature decreases with height in the atmosphere. Therefore, a high plateau, or mountainous region, is likely to be cooler than nearby areas at lower elevations. Relief has a unique affect on climate as well. In mountainous areas a **rain shadow** effect may be noticed. The rain shadow effect refers to the fact that the windward sides of mountains tend to be very rainy, while the leeward sides are often quite dry.

Ocean currents play a role in global heat transfer, bringing warmth to some areas, and cool temperatures to others. For example, the Gulf Stream is a major ocean current that flows from the Gulf of Mexico, along the U.S. east coast, to northwestern Europe. This current brings with it warm, moist air, accounting for Britain's rainy climate, and temperatures that are well above average for other locations at the same latitude.

The direction of an area's **prevailing winds** helps determine its climate as well. Winds that blow from the sea to inland areas tend to carry a significant amount of moisture, resulting in a rainy climate. Conversely, winds originating from a large landmass tend to be drier, bringing less precipitation to an area.

An area's **distance from the sea** significantly affects its climate. As a general rule, coastal areas tend to be milder and moister than inland areas. Inland areas tend to have hotter summers and colder winters than coastal areas.

Skill 10.2   Identify the causes and effects of climate changes throughout Earth's history.

Earth's climate has varied significantly throughout time, from glacial periods to interglacial periods. During glacial periods, ice covered significant portions of the planet. During interglacial periods, ice was confined to the poles, or had melted entirely. During interglacial periods, sea levels are higher and temperatures are milder. During glacial periods, sea levels are lower and temperatures are cooler—sometimes significantly so.

There are several proposed mechanisms for pre-industrial (natural) climate change:

Orbital properties: Changes in the shape of Earth's orbit (eccentricity), along with tilt and precession, affect the amount of sunlight the planet receives. These processes change according to cycles—100,000 years for eccentricity, 41,000 years for tilt, and 19,000-23,000 years for precession. According to a theory developed by Mulitin Milankovitch, a Serbian mathematician, these cycles can explain the occurrence of periodic ice ages.

Intensity of the Sun: Another theory holds that changes occurring within the Sun may be responsible for climate change. Changes in the Sun can affect the amount of sunlight Earth receives, and this mechanism may have caused the "Little Ice Age"—a period of reduced global temperatures that began in about 1450 A.D.

Volcanic activity: Periods of increased volcanic eruptions have also been linked with climate change. Increased volcanic activity leads to the emission of aerosols and carbon dioxide. Aerosols temporarily block sunlight and may contribute to short-term cooling. Carbon dioxide is a greenhouse gas, and its emission from increased volcanic activity may have contributed to past climate changes.

Today, human activities provide a new mechanism for climate change. The emission of greenhouse gases from human activities may be responsible for a significant amount of global warming due to an increased greenhouse effect. Increased global temperatures may result in higher sea levels, more severe storms, flooding, an increase in heat waves and drought, and the loss of species; effects will vary by region.

Skill 10.3   Assess how the cycling of carbon, energy, and water between the geosphere, hydrosphere, and atmosphere affects climate.

The cycling of materials through the geosphere, hydrosphere, and atmosphere plays a role in affecting climate.

Carbon is cycled through the geosphere, hydrosphere, biosphere, and atmosphere as part of the carbon cycle. Much of Earth's carbon originates as carbon dioxide outgassing from mid-ocean ridges. This carbon ends up in the atmosphere (as carbon dioxide), dissolved in the oceans, stored in biomass, and/or bound up in carbonate rocks. The main way in which the cycling of carbon affects climate is the contribution of carbon dioxide to the greenhouse effect. However, the natural carbon cycle has several feedback mechanisms that keep it in balance, maintaining temperatures within a given range. Excess carbon dioxide in the atmosphere due to human activity, however, may be causing global warming.

The cycling of heat energy affects climate as well. Earth's heat is derived from the Sun. It is transported to different areas of the planet via atmospheric and ocean currents. These currents are in part responsible for determining the climate of a given area. (See Skills 9.5 and 9.9 for further discussion of atmospheric energy transfer and ocean currents.)

The water cycle also plays in important role in climate determination. As part of the water cycle, water vapor is stored in the atmosphere. This water vapor forms clouds and precipitation, affecting weather and climate around the globe. Additionally, water vapor in the atmosphere is a greenhouse gas, and increased amounts of water vapor in the atmosphere lead to warmer conditions. (See Skill 4.4 for further discussion of the water cycle.)

Skill 10.4   Determine the effects of climate phenomena (e.g., monsoons, jet streams, El Niño).

Monsoons are huge wind systems that cover large geographic areas and that reverse direction seasonally. The monsoons of India and Asia are examples of these seasonal winds. They are responsible for the change between wet and dry seasons. During certain months of the year, winds blow from land to the ocean, which makes the air dry. However, when the wind switches direction, and blows ashore from the ocean, it brings with it monsoonal rains. These prolonged, heavy rains cause annual flooding in India, Bangladesh, and Pakistan. On the other hand, if the monsoon rains are late, or the season ends prematurely, these areas can suffer severe droughts.

Jet streams are narrow bands of fast moving air. They occur in the upper layers of the atmosphere, and the winds generally blow from west to east. Jet streams follow the boundary between warm air and cold air, and are strongest in the winter. Jet streams have a significant effect on the weather because they propel weather patterns forward with their flow. In addition to steering storms, jet stream winds influence the location of high and low pressure zones.

El Niño is a reverse of the normal weather patterns in the Pacific. A low-pressure area normally sits in the Pacific Ocean west of Hawaii and a high-pressure area normally sits off of the California coast. When an El Niño forms, these pressure areas shift eastward, causing the low-pressure area to be situated below Hawaii and the high-pressure area to move inland over California. Because of the shift in pressure areas, an El Niño affects the wind patterns (especially the jet stream and trade winds), and creates a wide variety of effects, including a direct impact on commercial fishing.

Normally, there is a shallow warm water layer over the colder, deeper waters along the coastlines. The temperature disparity causes an upwelling of rich nutrients from the lower layers of the cold water, creating a feeding zone that attracts a variety of marine life forms. In an El Niño situation, the warm water layer increases in both area coverage and depth. It extends downward, blocking the nutrient rich upwelling from reaching the feeding zone. Although many species can migrate to more friendly waters, some have limited mobility and die. The fishery area can become permanently barren depending on the intensity, duration, and repetition of El Niño events. Other effects of El Niño include:

Direct Effects
In the west: fires and drought.
In the east: rain, landslides, and fish migration.

Indirect Effects:
Greater chance of hurricanes in Hawaii.
Lesser chance of hurricanes in Virginia because of weakened trade winds.
Less rain during September and October.
Coastal erosion in the western states.
Fewer snow storms in the Cascades (Washington and Oregon).
The jet streams are altered as the high-pressure areas move.

A **La Niña** is the opposite of El Niño. However, it does not have as great an effect. It causes the east to be wetter and the west to be drier. Many scientists believe that both of these conditions are caused by a change in the surface temperature of the water of the Pacific Ocean.

Skill 10.5   Identify how climate changes may affect Florida's surface features, weather patterns, and biological diversity.

Surface Features

As sea level rises, Florida's coastal and low-lying areas may become inundated. A sea level rise of only a few meters would likely inundate the Florida Keys, cause significant flooding in the Everglades, and cover low lying coastal areas along both of Florida's coasts.

Biological Diversity

Florida's forests will be affected by warmer global temperatures. The geographic range of species could change, as could the health of forests in general. If the climate also becomes drier, Florida's forests could be replaced by grasslands; if conditions are warmer and wetter, more tropical species would come to dominate the forests. The mixed conifer/hardwood forests in the northern part of Florida would probably move northward, being replaced by tropical forests and/or dry tropical savanna. Additionally, rising temperatures and accompanying sea level rise threaten the Big Cypress Swamp, the Everglades, and the Florida Keys.

Weather Patterns

Higher global temperatures could bring more (or more intense) extreme weather events to Florida. Coupled with a higher sea level, this may result in more severe flooding, storm surges, and erosion. It is also likely that higher temperatures and drier conditions will result in more wildfires.

COMPETENCY 11.0   KNOWLEDGE OF ASTRONOMICAL OBJECTS AND PROCESSES

Skill 11.1   Identify the characteristics (e.g., mass, composition, location) of the major and minor objects in the solar system.

Our solar system consists of the Sun, planets, comets, meteors, and asteroids.

Object	Location	Mass (kg)	Diameter (km)	Composition	Characteristics
Sun	center of the solar system	2×10^{30}	1,390,000	gaseous, 94% hydrogen, lesser amounts of helium, 0.1% other elements	extremely hot; provides light, heat, and other energy to Earth; relatively young star
Mercury	closest planet to the Sun	3.3×10^{23}	4,897	solid, rocky, interior mantle and iron core	dry, hot, almost airless, extremely hot by day, extremely cold at night, craters, no moons
Venus	second planet from the Sun	4.865×10^{24}	12,100	solid, not much known about surface composition, iron/nickel core	mountains, canyons, valleys; extreme heat; thick clouds of sulfuric acid, no moons
Earth	third planet from the Sun	5.97×10^{24}	12,756	solid, oxygen, silicon, aluminum, iron, calcium, sodium, potassium, magnesium	atmosphere, supports life, abundant water, active plate tectonics, one moon
Mars	fourth planet from the Sun	6.42×10^{23}	6,792	solid, basalt, andesite, peridotite, iron, nickel, sulfur	mountains, valleys, polar ice, reddish dust, volcanoes, craters, possibility of life, two moons
Jupiter	fifth planet from the Sun	1.88×10^{27}	142,984	gaseous, mostly hydrogen and helium, possible small rocky core	cloud-covered, Great Red Spot (storm), cold at top of clouds, extremely high pressure lower down, 3 thin rings, 16 moons
Saturn	sixth planet from the Sun	5.68×10^{26}	120,536	gaseous, hydrogen and helium, solid inner core of iron and rocky metal, outer core of ammonia, methane and water	cloud-covered, cold at top of clouds, possible internal heat source, rings composed of ice particles, at least 30 moons

Uranus	seventh planet from the Sun	8.683×10^{25}	51,118	gas and liquid, hydrogen and methane, possible rocky core	tilted orbit, pale blue-green clouds, very cold in atmosphere, very hot in ocean and core, rings, 21 moons
Neptune	eighth planet from the Sun	1.024×10^{26}	49,532	gas and liquid, hydrogen, helium, methane, water, silicates, rock and ice core	thick cloud layer, blue in color, rings, 11 moons
Pluto	beyond Neptune	1.32×10^{22}	2300	not much known, frozen methane, thin methane atmosphere	dwarf planet, located in the Kuiper Belt, at some point in its orbit it is closer to the Sun than Neptune, one moon
Comets	originate in Kuiper Belt	variable	variable	ice chunks, frozen gasses, rock and dust	originate in Kuiper Belt, as comets near the Sun, they warm up; ice changes to gas and glows; released gas and dust forms glowing tail
Asteroids	asteroid belt, between Mars and Jupiter	variable	variable	rocky fragments	revolve around the Sun in the, sometimes effects of Jupiter or Mars change their orbits, can impact other planets including Earth
Meteors	variable	variable	variable	bits of rocky material falling through Earth's atmosphere	heated and glow because of friction of air, in space they are called meteoroids, in Earth's atmosphere they are called meteors, pieces that reach Earth's surface are called meteorites

Comparison of the Basic Characteristics of the Inner and Outer Planets:

INNER PLANETS	OUTER PLANETS
Referred to as the Terrestrial Planets	Called the Gas Giants or Jovian Planets
Similar to density to Earth	Very large in size.
Also referred to as the "Rocky Planets"	Primarily composed of gas.
Relatively small in size.	Less dense than Earth.
Spin slowly on their axis.	Rotate rapidly on their axis.
Few if any, moons.	Lots of moons.
Mercury	Jupiter
Venus	Saturn (Ringed)
Earth	Uranus
Mars	Neptune
+ Asteroid Belt	

Skill 11.2   Identify types and characteristics of deep space objects (e.g., quasars, galaxies, pulsars, black holes).

Quasars are very distant interstellar object less than one-light year in diameter that emits an extremely large quantity of energy in the form of electromagnetic radio waves. Quasars have puzzled astronomers for decades but it wasn't until the mid-1960's that astronomers made an astonishing discovery that started to unravel the mystery. These perplexing objects emitted energy primarily as radio waves rather the visible light, as is the case of most stars. Further investigations into the next decade revealed that these quasi-stellar objects (hence, quasars) were actually twin lobed radio sources.

Only about 3 percent of the 8,000 quasars so far discovered are actively emitting, but the modern theory about their origin suggests that they represent still active galaxies, billions of light-years distant from Earth.

Quasars show a tremendous redshift indicating that they are moving away from Earth. If so, their brilliance gives some indication of the energy involved, 10 to 100 times more than most galaxies.

Galaxies are large groups of billions of stars held together by mutual gravitational attraction. If you look into the night sky you may see a ribbon of stars packed so densely together that it appears to be a starlight cloud. You are looking at **the Milky Way Galaxy**, the galaxy in which our solar system is located. This ribbon of brilliance in the night is actually a collection of over 180 billion stars and a huge volume of interstellar dust and gasses.

You may also notice that there are groups of stars that appear closer together. These are **globular clusters**: a tightly grouped, high concentration of stars. These spherically arranged masses of stars are believed to be the oldest stars in the galaxy, approximately 10-20 billion years old. Each of the clusters contains between 10,000 to 1,000,000 individual stars and virtually no interstellar dust.

Although not the prevalent form, a spherical arrangement of stars is not uncommon. The Milky Way Galaxy is a **spiral galaxy**: a grouping of stars arranged in a thin, disk, spiraling geometric pattern, which has a central pivot point (nucleus) and arms radiating outward on which stars rotate around the nucleus, somewhat suggestive of the shape of a pinwheel. It is approximately 100,000 light-years in diameter and 2,000 light-years thick at the center, decreasing to 1,000 light-years at the edges.

In the late 1700's early astronomers studied hazy objects in the sky that weren't stars. However, it wasn't until the 1850's that telescopes became powerful enough to discern that the hazy objects had a spiraling structure. Almost a hundred years would pass before their identity was solved. In 1924, American astronomer Edwin Hubble determined that the objects were farther away than previously thought. This meant that for us to even see them, that they must have a greater luminosity than a single star. The conclusion was obvious; the objects were other galaxies, each composed of billions of stars.

Galaxies are named for their shapes as observed from Earth.

Spiral galaxy: As the name implies, the arrangement of the stars forms a spherical pattern. Spiral galaxies usually contain a great deal of interstellar gasses and dust.

Irregular galaxy: There is no discernable pattern in the arrangement of the stars. Like a spiral galaxy, irregular galaxies tend to have a large volume of interstellar gasses and dust.

Barred galaxy: The shape of this type of galaxy suggests a straight center core of stars joined by two or more relatively straight arms. About 30% of all galaxies are barred.

Elliptical galaxy: The pattern of this type of galaxy centers on an elliptical shaped central mass of stars, with other stars above or below the center, giving the entire mass an overall ovoid appearance. They contain virtually no dust or gasses and rotate very slowly, if at all. Most galaxies are elliptical.

The distance from Earth to other galaxies varies. The two closest galaxies, the *Large*, and *Small Magellanic Cloud,* are approximately 170,000 light-years away. As vast a distance as that may seem, it pales in comparison to the distance to the *Great Spiral Galaxy* which is two million light-years away.

A **pulsar** is a neutron star—the imploded core of a massive star after a supernova explosion—that emits radiation. Pulsars represent the end of a star's evolution. As the pulsar rotates, beams of radiation sweep into space similar to a lighthouse beacon. Since first discovered in 1967, over 350 pulsars have been catalogued.

Black holes represent the end of the evolution of stars at least 10 to 15 times as massive as the Sun. After a supernova explosion, the remainder of the massive star will collapse in on itself to the point of zero volume and infinite density. Once infinite density is reached, no light ever escapes the star, so it is known as a black hole.

A **nebula** is a cloud of dust and gas that may be lit up by the light of a nearby star or stars. Some nebulae are where new stars are formed; others are formed when a star's life ends.

Skill 11.3   Interpret the Hertzsprung-Russell diagram with regard to stellar evolution and star characteristics.

Scientists believe that **stars** form when compression waves traveling through clouds of gas (nebulae) create knots of gas in the clouds. The force of gravity within these denser areas then attracts gas particles. As the knot grows, the force increases and attracts more gas particles, eventually forming a large sphere of compressed gas with internal temperatures reaching a few million degrees celsius. At these temperatures, the gases in the knot become so hot that nuclear fusion of hydrogen takes place forming helium, creating large amounts of nuclear energy and forming a new star. Pressure from the radiation of these new stars causes more knots to form in the gas cloud, initiating the process of creating more stars.

All stars derive their energy through the thermonuclear fusion of light elements into heavy elements. The minimum temperature required for the fusion of hydrogen is 5 million degrees. Elements with more protons in their nuclei require higher temperatures. For instance, to fuse carbon requires a temperature of about 1 billion degrees.

A star that is composed of mostly hydrogen is a young star. As a star gets older its hydrogen is consumed and tremendous energy and light is released through fusion. This is a three-step process:

(1) two hydrogen nuclei (protons) fuse to form a heavy hydrogen called deuterium and release an electron and 4.04 MeV energy,
(2) the deuterium fuses with another hydrogen nucleus (proton) to form a helium-3 and release a neutron and 3.28 MeV energy, and
(3) and the helium-3 fuses with another helium-3 to form a helium-4 and release two hydrogen atoms and 10.28 MeV energy.

In stars with central temperatures greater than 600-700 million degrees, carbon fusion is thought to take over the dominant role rather than hydrogen fusion. Carbon fusions can produce magnesium, sodium, neon, or helium. Some of the reactions release energy and alpha particles or protons.

Characteristics of Stars

Not all stars are alike. Their energy outputs vary from 111,000th of the Sun's energy to 100,000 times the energy of Earth's Sun. The laws of physics tell us that the more energy an object has, the hotter it is. They also relate color to temperature. Therefore, by observing the color of a star, we get information about its temperature.

The Hertzsprung-Russell Diagram

In 1913 American astronomer Henry Norris Russell and Danish astronomer Ejnar Hertzsprung theorized that the energy emitted by a star is directly related to the star's color. Their supporting graph is now known as the **Hertzsprung-Russell Diagram (H-R Diagram):** a graph that shows the relationship between a star's color, temperature, and mass.

On a H-R Diagram the majority (90%) of the stars plotted form a diagonal line called the **main sequence**: the region of the H-R Diagram running from top left to bottom right. Hot, blue stars are at the top left corner. Cooler, red stars are located at the bottom right. The middle of main sequence contains yellow stars such as the Sun.

Star mass is also shown on the H-R diagram, increasing from the bottom to the top of the main sequence.

The stars at the bottom right have masses about one-tenth of that of Earth's sun, and the masses increase until you reach the top left where there are stars with masses ten times greater than that of the Sun.

The truly large stars are called **supergiant stars**: exceptionally massive and luminous stars 10 to 1,000 times brighter than the Sun. The smallest stars are called **dwarf stars**: dying stars that have collapsed in size. Although small in size, dwarf stars are extremely dense. Although supergiants are extremely large, they may be less dense than Earth's outer atmosphere.

We can also use the H-R Diagram to illustrate the life cycle of stars.

Skill 11.4   Interpret the sequences and forces involved in the origin of the solar system.

Most cosmologists believe that Earth is the indirect result of a supernova. The thin cloud (planetary nebula) of gas and dust from which the Sun and its planets are formed, was struck by the shock wave and remnant matter from an exploded star(s) outside of our galaxy. In fact, the stars manufactured every chemical element heavier than hydrogen.

The turbulence caused by the shock wave caused our solar system to begin forming as it absorbed some of the heavy atoms flung outward in the supernova. Our solar system is composed mostly of matter assembled from a star or stars that disappeared billions of years ago.

Around five billion years ago our planetary nebulae spun faster as it condensed and material near the center contracted inward forming a proto-sun. As more materials came together, mass and consequently gravitational attraction increased, pulling in more mass. This cycle continued until the mass reached the point that nuclear fusion occurred and the Sun was born.

Concurrently, the proto-sun's gravitational mass pulled heavier, denser elements inward from the clouds of cosmic material that surrounded it. These elements eventually coalesced through the process of **accretion**: the clumping together of small particles into large masses- the planets of our solar system.

The period of accretion lasted approximately 50 to 70 million years, ceasing when the proto-Sun experienced nuclear fusion to become the Sun. The violence associated with this nuclear reaction swept through the inner planets, clearing the system of particles, ending the period of rapid accretion.

The closest planets received too much heat and, consequently, did not develop the planetary characteristics to support life as we know it. The farthest planets did not receive enough heat to sufficiently coalesce the gasses into solid form. Earth was the only planet in the perfect position to develop the conditions necessary to maintain life.

Skill 11.5   Identify the causes and effects of the cycles of the Earth-Moon-Sun system (e.g., seasons, tides, eclipses, precession, moon phases).

Seasonal Change

Seasonal change on Earth is caused by Earth's axial title. Because Earth's axis is tilted, different parts of the globe are tilted toward the Sun at different parts of the year. During either hemisphere's summer, the Sun's rays strike Earth's surface at a more direct angle, making for warmer conditions. During the winter, the Suns' rays strike the surface indirectly; therefore, the same amount of solar energy is distributed over a wider surface area, making for cooler conditions.

There are four key points on Earth's orbital path:
- Winter Solstice (December 21) = Shortest day of the year in the northern hemisphere.
- Summer Solstice (June 21) = Longest day of the year in the northern hemisphere.
- Vernal Equinox (March 21) = Marks the beginning of spring.
- Autumnal Equinox (Sept 21) = Marks the beginning of autumn.

These dates will vary slightly in relation to leap years. During the summer solstice, insolation is at a maximum in the northern hemisphere, and at a minimum in the southern hemisphere.

Tides

The periodic rise and fall of the liquid bodies on Earth are the direct result of the gravitational influence of the Moon and, to a much lesser extent, the Sun. Tides are produced by the differences between gravitational forces acting on parts of an object. The Moon's gravitational attraction causes the oceans on the Moon side to bulge out in that direction. Centrifugal force caused by Earth's movement around a center of gravity shared by the Moon results in a bulge on the side of the planet facing away from the Moon. Earth's rotation on its axis results in most places experiencing two high tides each day, as Earth rotates through each bulge.

Because of its distance from Earth, the Sun's gravitational effect on tides is only half that of the Moon's. However, when the gravitational effects of both the Sun and Moon join together during a new moon and a full moon phase, the tidal effects can be extreme. During a new moon and a full moon, tidal effects are much more pronounced as the tidal bulges join together to produce very high and very low tides. These pronounced types of tide are collectively known as **spring tides**. During the first and third quarters of the moon phases, the Sun's effect is negligible and consequently, the tides are lower. These are **neap tides**.

Eclipses

Eclipse: a phenomenon that occurs when a stellar body is shadowed by another and, as a result, is rendered invisible.

Earth, Moon, and Sun must be in perfect alignment with each other to result in either a lunar or solar eclipse.

- **Lunar Eclipse**: The shadow of Earth darkens the Moon. The Moon is in Earth's shadow.
- **Solar Eclipse**: The Moon is between the Sun and Earth. Earth is in the Moon's shadow.

A solar eclipse may be annular (partial) or total (full).

Annular: a type of solar eclipse in which the darkest part of the shadow (the umbra) doesn't touch Earth.

Total: a type of solar eclipse in which the darkest part of the shadow (the umbra) does touch Earth.

Umbra: the central region of the shadow caused by an eclipse. No light hits in this region. This is typically associated with total eclipses.

Penumbra: the lighter, outer edges of the shadow created during an eclipse. Some light hits in these regions. This is typically associated with annular (partial) eclipses.

Precession

Precession refers to a change in the orientation of Earth's rotational axis, much like a wobbling top's axis of rotation changes through time. Precession occurs because the gravitational forces of the Sun and Moon pull on Earth's equatorial bulge. This causes Earth to "wobble" as it spins. It takes approximately 26,000 years for Earth's rotational axis to make one complete revolution. Precession has an effect on the seasonal balance of radiation because it changes the timing of the equinoxes and of Earth's aphelion (point in Earth's orbit when it is farthest from the Sun) and perihelion (point in Earth's orbit when it is closest to the Sun).

Phases of the Moon

Just as Earth follows an orbit around the Sun, the Moon follows an eastward moving orbit around Earth. Because the Moon's rotational period matches Earth's and its' period of revolution is 27.3 days (called the **sidereal period**), this keeps one side of the Moon always facing Earth. The side always facing us is called the near side, and the darkened side we never see is called the far side.

Phases of the Moon: the apparent change in shape of the Moon caused by the absence or presence of reflected sunlight as the Moon orbits around Earth.

The orbital pattern of the Moon in relation to the Sun and Earth determines the extent of lunar illumination, and consequently, what illuminated shape is presented to Earth. When the moon is between the Sun and Earth, the side facing us is darkened, and we refer to this as a new moon. The opposite pattern occurs in the second half of the complete lunar cycle, when the Moon is fully illuminated and bright in the night sky. This is called a full moon. The other phases between these extremes reflect the orbital point of the Moon as it completes its journey around Earth.

Skill 11.6   Identify the physical properties of the Sun, its dynamic nature, and its effects on Earth systems.

The **Sun** is the nearest star to Earth, which produces solar energy. By the process of nuclear fusion, hydrogen gas is converted to helium gas. Energy flows out of the core to the surface, allowing radiation to escape into space.

Parts of the sun include:
- The **core:** the inner portion of the sun where fusion takes place
- The **photosphere:** the surface of the sun which produces **sunspots,** which are cool, dark areas that can be seen on its surface
- The **chromosphere:** hydrogen gas causes this portion to be red in color. Also found here are solar flares (sudden brightness of the chromosphere) and solar prominences (gases that shoot outward from the chromosphere).
- The **corona**, the transparent area of sun visible only during a total eclipse

The Sun's effect on Earth is significant. Heat energy in the form of solar radiation travels from the Sun to heat Earth's surface. This energy enables the planet to support life, drives Earth's weather systems, and affects climate. **Solar flares** release particles that travel toward Earth. These particles disturb radio reception and also affect the magnetic field on Earth.

Skill 11.7   Identify the matter and forces involved in the evolution of the universe (e.g., big bang theory)

The **Big Bang Theory** proposes that all the mass and energy of the universe was originally concentrated at a single geometric point and, for unknown reasons, experienced a massive explosion that scattered the matter throughout the universe. The concept of a massive explosion is supported by the distribution of background radiation and the measurable fact that the galaxies are moving away from each other at great speed.

The universe originated around 15 billion years ago with the "Big Bang," and continued to expand for the first 10 billion years. The universe was originally unimaginably hot, but around 1 million years after the Big Bang, it cooled enough to allow for the formation of atoms from the energy and particles.

Most of these atoms were hydrogen and they comprise the most abundant form of matter in the universe. Around a billion years after the Big Bang, the matter had cooled enough to begin congealing into the first stars and galaxies.

COMPETENCY 12.0   KNOWLEDGE OF SPACE EXPLORATION

Skill 12.1   Compare relative and absolute methods for measurement of astronomical distances.

Stars are generally a very far distance away from each other. The distances can be millions of kilometers, and as a result, the sheer scope of the distance can be difficult to comprehend. To ease this problem, astronomers utilize a series of different measurement scales to help place the distances in perspective.

Example: Imagine the Sun as a marble 1 cm in diameter. The next closest star, Proxima Centauri, would be over 300 kilometers away.

Measurement Units in Astronomy

Astronomical distances represent mind-boggling amounts of distance. Because our standard units of distance measurement (i.e. kilometers) would result in so large of a number as to become almost incomprehensible, physicists use different units of measurement to reference the vast distances involved in astronomy.

Within our solar system, the standard unit of distance measurement is the **AU (astronomical unit).** The **AU** is the mean distance between the Sun and Earth. 1 AU = 1.495979×10^{11} m. Outside of our solar system, the standard unit of distance measurement is the **parsec.** 1 parsec = 206,265 AU or 3.26 light years (LY).

Light year (LY): the distance light travels in one year. As the speed of light is 3.00×10^8 m/sec, one light year represents a distance of 9.5×10^{12} km, or 63,000 AU.

Measuring the Distance to the Stars

The distances are measured using a shift in viewpoint. This is called the **parallax:** an apparent change in the position of an object due to a change in the location of the observer. In astronomy, parallax is measured in seconds of arc. One second of arc = 1/3600 of a degree.

The concept of measuring distances by parallax is based on the mathematical discipline of trigonometry. Example: Photos of the distant stars are taken at different times, usually 6 months apart. The apparent shift in position that the star has moved in comparison to the previous photo is the parallax.

By measuring the angles, we can use trigonometric functions of sine, cosine, and tangent to determine a distance to the object. The smaller the parallax is, the greater the distance to the star.

Skill 12.2   Evaluate functions and benefits of the different types of ground- and space-based astronomical instruments (e.g., x-ray, optical, infrared, radio telescopes, spectrometers).

X-ray Astronomy

X-rays are part of the light spectrum, but cannot be detected by the naked eye. The energy of an x-ray photon is around 1000 times greater than that of a photon of visible light. Extremely hot objects emit x-rays, and astronomers can use x-rays to image the objects emitting them. X-ray astronomy relies on satellites, and can provide a wide range of data. X-ray data can provide information about galaxies, black holes, pulsars, the Sun, neutron stars, and much more.

Optical Telescopes

There are two main styles of optical telescopes: refractor and reflector.

Refraction: the bending of light. Example: Put a straw in a clear glass of water. Now look at straw through the side of the glass. It will appear to bend at the point where the straw enters the water.

Refractor telescopes are optical devices that make use of lenses to magnify and display received images. Professional astronomers do not use refractor telescopes because of two main problems. First the telescopes are affected by chromatic aberrations which make it difficult to focus on the stars. Second, because they rely solely on lenses, the telescopes have inherent weight and size restrictions. Chromatic aberrations are a problem because as the lenses split the light into its chromatic components; each color has a different focal point based on its wavelength. This causes details on the image to blur. To aid in this problem lenses with different refractive indexes (degrees of bending) are sandwiched together in order to compensate for the aberrations and properly focus on the image. However, this compensation method increases the size and weight of the telescope.

Reflector Telescopes

Reflection: the re-emission of light off of an object struck by the light.
Example: Look at yourself in the mirror. What your eyes see is the re-emission of light waves that have struck you and the mirror.

Reflector telescopes are optical devices that make use of a mirror or mirrors, to reflect light waves to an eyepiece (ocular), thereby eliminating chromatic aberrations. There are different types of reflector telescopes; some use mirrors only, and others make use of both lenses and mirrors.

The **objective** is the primary focus mirror in a reflector telescope and is usually curved. Any other mirrors in the telescope are referred to as secondary, tertiary, etc. depending on the number of mirrors present. On both refractor and reflector telescopes, the eyepiece is called the **ocular**. The most common style of reflector telescope used is the Schmidt-Cassegrain. The two major advantages of a reflector telescope over a refractor style telescope are:

- No chromatic aberrations results in a much clearer and detailed image than in a refractor telescope.

- Their smaller size makes them easier to use and they weigh less because they don't rely on the heavy, thick glass lenses required in a refractor type.

However, there are still limits to the size of a reflecting telescope. They are very expensive and it is an extremely difficult and slow process to grind the mirror to the proper specifications. The larger the mirror or mirrors required to view distant objects, the more likely it is that there will be **imperfections** in the mirror. Weight also becomes an issue depending on the size of the mirror required. The heavier and thicker the mirror required, the greater the chance that the mirror will sag, slightly distorting the image. Also, the mirror will heat and cool unevenly, causing further distortion.

Active optics: a type of optical device that is composed of hexagonal pieces of mirror whose positions are controlled by a computer. Also referred to as **active telescopes**.

Collectively, smaller pieces of mirror weigh less than a single large mirror and, more importantly, they generally do not suffer from sagging problems. Small hexagonal shaped pieces of mirror are arranged next to each other to form a larger reflection surface. Computer-controlled thrusters mounted underneath the pieces control the mirror position and focus. The use of the smaller pieces working in conjunction eliminates sagging and the uneven heating and cooling problems found in extremely large, single mirror telescopes.

Example: The Keck Telescope in Hawaii is able to have a 10-meter diameter reflective surface through the use of active optics. Similarly, the Hobby-Eberly Telescope composed of 91 hexagons has an 11-meter diameter reflective surface, making it the largest telescope on Earth.

New Generation Telescopes

The **Hubble Space Telescope** is named in honor of the American astronomer, Edwin Hubble, who proved the theory of an expanding universe. The Hubble Space Telescope, although only possessing a 2.4 meter diameter reflective surface, isn't affected by atmospheric constraints, and as a result, it provides a much clearer, higher resolution image of stellar objects than is possible through the use of an Earth-based telescope. Two companies competed in the design phase of manufacturing the telescope, and working models of each design were constructed. However, shortly after being positioned in space, the mirror on the winning design was discovered to have imperfections that produced a great deal of distortion in the received images. Initially, a solution for this problem seemed simple—place the losing contractor's design up in space in place of the flawed telescope. But a problem quickly arose. When NASA scientists contacted the second company, they were told that the losing model was no longer available. In any event, NASA eventually figured out a means to correct the imperfections and space shuttle astronauts successfully affected the repairs.

A **charged coupling device (CCD)** is a camera plate made up of thousands of tiny pixels. The pixels carry a slight electrical charge and when photons strike a pixel, electrons are released. This release of electrons causes a flow of current through an attached wire, and this current is detected by a computer chip and used to construct images based on the number of strikes. The number of strikes also shows the intensity of the received image.

CCD cameras have a wide range of applications besides astronomy. This type of technology is being successfully employed in many of the newest, high-resolution cameras available to the general public.

Infrared Astronomy

Infrared astronomy involves the detection of infrared radiation (heat energy) emitted from objects in space. It can be used to study just about any object in the universe, since every object that has a temperature emits infrared radiation. Infrared astronomy is useful because it allows astronomers to view objects hidden from optical telescopes, which may be hidden by gas and dust.

Radio Telescopes

Variances in radio waves received from space can be translated into usable astronomical data. The advantages offered by use of radio telescopes are many: it's cheaper to build a radio telescope than optical telescopes, they can operate 24 hours a day and be built just about anywhere on Earth, and they open up an entirely new window of space investigation. They initially had one major disadvantage: the useable radio waves received from space were not overly abundant and generally very weak, and you needed a huge receiving dish to detect the signals. To overcome these problems, scientists developed a technique called radio interferometry.

Radio interferometry: a method of amplifying weak radio waves by assembling (in a Y-shaped pattern) a series of small radio telescopes all pointed at the same point in the sky. The telescopes add their received signals together to form an overlay of signals. Computers control the angle of incidence and correlate the incoming signals. This improves resolution and limits the size of the radio telescope dish needed for a single unit.

Spectroscopy

Spectroscopy involves the study of light emitted by an object. **Spectrometers** are used to separate light out into its individual wavelengths, which creates a light spectrum. An object's spectrum can reveal much about its composition, temperature, density, and motion, so spectroscopy is a very useful tool in astronomy.

Skill 12.3   Interpret electromagnetic spectra and radiation intensity data from astronomical objects.

Electromagnetic spectrum: the ordered pattern produced when light or other electromagnetic radiation is split into its wavelength components. For visible light emissions, the splitting is usually accomplished through the use of a prism or diffraction grating. Example: A prism splits white light into its various colored components.

Visible light spectrum: that portion of the electromagnetic spectrum in which the components can be detected by the human eye. The visible light spectrum makes up only a very small portion of the electromagnetic spectrum.

Examining the Visible Light Spectrum

We use a **spectrograph** or **spectroscope** to examine the visible light spectra of an object. A basic spectroscope is composed of a barrier (with an aperture), a prism, and a screen. The aperture in the barrier focuses the light onto the prism, which splits the received light into its spectrum components and displays it on the screen.

Spectroscopy: the study of the spectrum.

Spectra: the emitted electromagnetic or visible light line pattern produced by an object. There are three different types of spectra: continuous, absorption, and emission.

Continuous spectrum: light from a glowing source. Example: A prismatic rainbow. All the colors that comprise the white light are received.

Absorption spectrum: a continuous colored spectrum, interrupted by dark lines.

Emission spectrum: a continuous, dark spectrum interrupted by lines of color. The lines of color appear to be slices of the continuous spectrum.

The received spectra are unique to each element and act as the "fingerprints" of the element. By observing the spectra, we can determine a star's temperature and elemental composition. If the lines are shifted, we can determine how far and at what speed the star is moving. We do this by comparing the star's spectral emissions to known data for various earthly elements.

Kirchoff's Laws are a means of determining the chemical characteristics of the source of the spectral lines and are directly related to the properties of atoms.

Continuous spectrum: The source must be a very dense solid or liquid. Example: The filament in a light bulb.

Absorption spectrum: The source must be a continuous spectrum source behind a layer of cool, thin gas. Example: Our Sun.

Emission spectrum: The source must be a very hot, low-density gas. Example: fluorescent or neon light bulbs.

An atom is composed of a nucleus that contains positively charged protons, neutrally charged neutrons, and an electron shell that holds a varying number of negatively charged electrons. The electrons orbit around the nucleus (ground state), and as they absorb energy, they move to a new position on the outer orbits of the electron shell. They are said to be "excited." The amount of energy absorbed by an electron will determine the orbit level it will follow. As the electron loses energy, it attempts to return to its ground state and sheds **photons**, quantum particles of electromagnetic energy that carry an amount of energy that depends upon its wavelength.

As the electron returns toward ground state, it gives off a different wavelength. Each wavelength has its own unique characteristics. Some wavelengths absorb some colors and reemit others. This is why the hottest stars look bluer than cooler stars. The elements comprising the star are absorbing the red color wavelengths and re-emitting the blue color wavelengths.

We compare received data to known data and apply Kirchhoff's Laws to determine the type of gas and materials of which the star is composed.

Celestial Brightness

Over 2,000 years ago the Greek astronomer Hipparchus devised a system to classify the brightness of the stars. He ranked the brightest stars as first-class stars, the next brightest as second-class, etc., down to the faintest stars, the sixth-class. Although this system worked well for millennia, with the advent of more powerful telescopes, astronomers discovered stars that were both brighter and fainter than the brightest and faintest stars in the star catalog. To solve this problem, modern astronomers extended the magnitude system into negative numbers to account for the brighter stars. Example: Sirius, the brightest star in the sky, has a magnitude of -1.42.

These numbers represent a star's **apparent visual magnitude (m_v):** a star's brightness as seen from Earth. On the magnitude scale, the larger the number, the fainter the star.

The relative brightness of the stars in a particular constellation is denoted by the use of lower case Greek letters; the star appearing brightest in the constellation being Alpha (α) and the star appearing faintest being Omega (ω). The Greek alphabet symbols are used as a prefix appended to the constellation's name. The possessive form of the name is used, and this is created by appending the suffix 'is' to the name of the constellation. Example: The brightest star in the constellation Orion is noted as α Orionis = Alpha Orionis.

However, stellar brightness requires a more precise measurement system beyond the original model because variances in the human eye and weather conditions can dramatically affect the apparent magnitude of a star.

For the purposes of mathematical measurement astronomers use a star's **intensity**, a measure of the light energy from a star that hits 1 square meter in 1 second.

We can use this modem system in conjunction with the Hipparchus devised brightness classifications because a difference of 5 magnitudes corresponds to a intensity ratio of 100. This allows us to compare the intensity of one star to another based on the mathematical progression of the difference in magnitude.

Skill 12.4   Identify significant manned and unmanned space exploration events, programs, and objectives.

Planetary Exploration

One of the primary means of learning more about the planetary bodies of the solar system is through space exploration. In the United States, space exploration began in the 1960's when the first probes journeyed toward Earth's Moon.

The Outer Planets

Pioneer 10 and 11 visited Jupiter in the early 1970's.
Voyager 1 visited Jupiter and Titan (a Moon of Saturn).
Voyager 2 visited Jupiter, Saturn, Uranus, Neptune, and then exited the solar system. Voyager 2 is the only probe to visit all 4 of the Jovian planets.

Recent Explorations

Galileo: Launched in 1989, Galileo is currently orbiting Jupiter.
Cassini-Huygens: Launched in 1997, it reached Saturn in 2004.
Cassini is the spacecraft that orbits Saturn. Huygens is the probe that reached Saturn's moon Titan in 2005.

Titan was chosen because it has an atmosphere and other probes have detected possible water phases. Additionally, Titan's density indicates it's more Earth-like than Saturn. Given the possibility of water and a solid surface, conditions may exist to support some form of life.

Stardust: Launched in 1998, the mission was to collect material from the comet Wild 2 and its coma. It returned in 2006. This mission marked the first time that collected physical specimens have been returned to Earth from a location other than the Moon.

Mercury

Mercury was visited in the early 1970's.

Mariner 10 probe: Launched in November 1973, the probe reached Mercury in 1974. It orbited the planet three times, collecting basic photographic data. Since the initial visit, no other probes have been sent there.

Venus

Venus has had lots of exploration, visited primarily during the 1960's and 1970's. Twelve probes have been sent there.

- Mariner 4, 5, and 10 (conducted orbital recon)
- Venera 4, 7, 12, 15, and 16 from the Soviet Union (mostly orbital recon)
- Venera 7 actually landed on the surface of Venus.
- Pioneer (orbital recon)
- Magellan produced the most recent and accurate data. Venus's surface is very hot. Electronics have trouble surviving the heat and this limits attempts to land.

Mars

Visited in the late 1960's, early 1970's, and then again in the 1990's.

Viking 1 and 2. Viking 1 actually landed on the surface. It was the first probe on Mars.
Pathfinder & Sojourner: Sojourner actually probed the surface with a small remote controlled robotic all terrain vehicle.

The Moon

The Moon was the first celestial object to be flown by, orbited, and landed upon. It is thus far the only object to have been visited by astronauts. The Apollo missions in the 1960s explored the Moon. Apollo 8 orbited the moon and Apollo 11 landed men on the Moon.

Dwarf Planets

The New Horizons mission launched in 2006 and is currently on its way to Pluto. It is estimated to near Pluto in 2015, at which point it will continue on into the Kuiper Belt to search for other Kuiper Belt objects.

Skill 12.5 Identify the historical development of astronomy based on the contributions of Aristotle, Ptolemy, Copernicus, Brahe, Kepler, Galileo, Newton, Einstein, and Hubble.

Aristotle

Aristotle (384-322 BC), a Greek philosopher, student of Plato, and teacher himself, believed in a geocentric universe composed of four elements (earth, air, water, and fire). He believed that the stationary Earth was surrounded by stars on a large, black sphere. Between the sphere of the stars and Earth itself, he believed there existed several crystalline spheres that held one planet each (the Sun, the Moon, Mercury, Venus, Mars, Jupiter, and Saturn).

Ptolemy

Ptolemy (~85-165 AD) was an astronomer, geographer, and mathematician. He developed a mathematical model to explain the motions of the solar system based on the geocentric model.

Nicolaus Copernicus

Nicolaus Copernicus (1473-1543), a mathematician and astronomer, was the first to successfully propose a heliocentric model for the solar system. (The first ideas about the Sun being at the center of the solar system date back to around the third century BCE, but were not taken seriously until Copernicus.) He believed that the size of a planet's orbit was directly related to its distance from the Sun. He also proposed that Earth rotated every 24 hours on its axis, causing the stars to appear to revolve around Earth. His ideas were controversial at first, but the basic heliocentric model has stood the test of time.

Tycho Brahe

Danish astronomer Tycho Brahe (1546-1501) played an integral role in the history of astronomy. He proposed a new model of the solar system (that had Earth at the center) that was intermediate between the Ptolemaic and Coperincan models. He also designed, built, and calibrated astronomical instruments, and changed the way celestial objects were observed. Rather than observe the positions of plants and moons at specific points in their orbits, Brahe observed objects throughout their orbits, which lead to the discovery of various orbital anomalies. His discoveries and observations paved the way for the work of Johannes Kepler.

Kepler's Law of Planetary Motion

Danish astronomer Johannes Kepler (1571-1630) postulated what are now known as Kepler's Laws of Planetary Motion.

Kepler's First Law of Planetary Motion: A planet can't travel in a circle. A planet travels along an elliptical path, with the Sun at one focal point.

Kepler's Second Law of Planetary Motion: Planets must sweep out equal areas, at equal amounts of time, on these elliptical paths. When a planet is nearer to the Sun on the planet's elliptical path, it must move faster to sweep over the same area.

Kepler's Third Law of Planetary Motion: A planet's orbital period squared is proportional to its average distance from the Sun cubed ($a3 = p2$).
Example: Jupiter's average distance to the Sun is 5.20 AU. If a equals 5.20 AU, then a3 equals 140.6 AU. Therefore, the orbital period of Jupiter must be the square root of 140.6, which equals a period of about 11.8 light-years.

The significance of Kepler's Laws is that they overthrew the ancient concept of uniform circular motion, which was a major support for the geocentric theory.

Kepler suggested that the eccentricity of the planetary motion could be mathematically summarized as $e=c/a$. The two major points on the elliptical orbit are the perihelion and aphelion.

- **Perihelion**: the closest point of approach to the Sun on the elliptical path. This is the point at which the planet travels the fastest in keeping with Kepler's 2nd Law.
- **Aphelion**: the farthest point away from the Sun on the elliptical path. This is the point at which the planet travels the slowest in keeping with Kepler's 2nd Law.

Although Kepler postulated the three laws of planetary motion, he was never able to explain why the planets move along their elliptical orbits, only that they did.

Galileo

Galileo Galilei (1564-16342 AD) was an Italian astronomer and inventor who built his first telescope in 1609. Contrary to popular myth, Galileo didn't invent the telescope but, using existing plans, gradually improved upon the design. Acknowledged today as the "Father of Experimental Science," Galileo developed a careful, methodical approach to observation and collection of data on planetary motion. His conclusions eventually changed the entire direction of astronomical thought and theory.

Galileo's Observations

The Moon is not flat and it has holes on its surface. The significance of Earth-like features meant that the Moon wasn't perfect. At that time, Greek philosophy accepted that all things in the heavens were perfect. Galileo saw stars that were not visible to the naked eye. In observing Venus, he saw the phases of the planet. In observing Jupiter, Galileo saw four moons rotating around the planet. Galileo saw sunspots on the Sun. Galileo's observations proved the heliocentric model was correct and supported Kelper's theory of planetary motion. The major significance of Galileo's observations is that they totally disproved the geocentric model of the universe, and thereby destroyed the 2,000 year old Aristotelian vision of the universe.

Isaac Newton

Isaac Newton (1642-1727) was an English physicist and mathematician. Newton developed his three laws of motion, and demonstrated how Kepler's laws of planetary motion could be explained by these new laws. Additionally, he showed that Kepler's laws were only partially correct, and amended them himself.

A major contribution by Newton was his Law of Gravitation, which states that every object attracts every other object with a force that for any two objects is directly proportional to the mass of each object. In simpler terms, objects with mass attract one another.

Newton also invented the reflecting telescope using mirrors to gather light rays on a curved mirror which produces a small focused image and provided a scientific explanation for the tides.

Albert Einstein

Albert Einstein (1879-1955) was a German-American physicist. His Theories of Special and General Relativity changed the way we think about the universe. The Theory of Special Relativity states that nothing can move faster than the speed of light, and that time and distance measurements are relative to the observer's frame of reference. The theory views space-time as a single phenomenon, in fact. It also states that mass can be converted into energy, and vice versa. General relativity expands the ideas of the special relativity theory to include gravity and acceleration.

Edwin Hubble

Edwin Hubble (1889-1953) was an American astronomer who drastically changed our view of space. Hubble discovered that he Milky Way is just one of millions of galaxies and that the universe itself is expanding. His ideas provided the first evidence for the Big Bang Theory, and he is often credited with being the father of cosmology.

Skill 12.6   Evaluate the cultural and economic effects of the space program in Florida.

The eastern coast of central Florida has been home to various aspects of the U.S. space program since the 1950s when it was first used as a missile launch site by the Air Force. Florida's role in the space program was solidified when NASA built the massive Kennedy Space Center, which has had a lasting effect on the region. The initiation of the space program lead to an explosion in the population of Brevard County, and the space program became a cornerstone of the economy. Throughout the history of the space program, as various projects ran their course, employment levels have fluctuated. Tourism and small, non-space-related businesses were encouraged to balance out the economy. The space program still has a significant part in Florida's culture and economy. More than just a source of jobs in the region, the space program is responsible for drawing tourists to the region, strengthening the tourism industry and aiding local businesses.

Sample Test

Directions: The following are multiple choice questions. Select from each grouping the best answer.

1. In which layer of the atmosphere would you expect most weather to occur?

A. troposphere
B. thermosphere
C. mesosphere

2. Which is the final stage in scientific inquiry?

A. observing
B. classifying
C. communication

3. Which layer of Earth's atmosphere contains the ozone layer?

A. thermosphere
B. troposphere
C. stratosphere

4. Which is the name for the model of the solar system developed by Copernicus?

A. stellar
B. heliocentric
C. geocentric

5. Qualitative research ends with

A. laws
B. hypotheses and theories
C. observations

6. The National Science Teacher's Association recommends limiting science classes to _____ or fewer students.

A. 18
B. 20
C. 24

7. A star's light and heat are produced by

A. magnetism
B. electricity
C. nuclear fusion

8. The goal of the TOPEX/Poseidon mission was to

A. monitor weather conditions
B. examine the ozone layer
C. map ocean surface topography

9. Rapid diversification of fish occurred in the

A. Cambrian
B. Devonian
C. Pliocene

10. Which type of reef is a coral island with a central lagoon?

A. fringing reef
B. barrier reef
C. atoll

11. Which is an example of a model?

A. ultraviolet radiation
B. the rock cycle
C. global warming

12. Air flows from areas of _____ pressure to areas of _____ pressure.

A. high, low
B. low, high
C. high, high

13. When molecules in the air cool and combine to form rain, _____ has occurred.

A. condensation
B. convection
C. radiation

14. On a weather map, lines indicating constant pressure are called

A. isotherms
B. isodrosotherms
C. isobars

15. Florida's karst terrain is a result of

A. carbonate bedrock
B. heavy rainfall
C. proximity to the ocean

16. A yardang is formed by the erosive power of

A. wind
B. water
C. ice

17. On a topographic map, the points of a V representing a stream point

A. downstream
B. upstream
C. perpendicular to the stream

18. When the Sun, the Moon and Earth are aligned, what type of tide is produced?

A. neap tide
B. high tide
C. spring tide

19. North of the equator, currents move in which direction?

A. counter-clock wise
B. clockwise
C. northerly

20. Rocks that serve as aquifers are

A. impermeable
B. permeable
C. igneous

21. A narrow piece of land that juts out into the water is known as a

A. cape
B. delta
C. atoll

22. The expansion of desert-like conditions into adjacent areas is

A. erosion
B. desertification
C. urbanization

23. Earth's outer core is probably

A. liquid
B. solid
C. rocky

24. If a geologist uses the principle of superposition to date a sequence of rocks, this is an example of

A. absolute dating
B. relative dating
C. dendrochronology

25. The San Andreas fault is classified as a

A. transform fault
B. spreading center
C. subduction zone

26. The New Horizons mission is currently on its way to

A. the Sun
B. Mars
C. Pluto

27. Most of Florida's groundwater comes from

A. the Everglades
B. the Biscayne Aquifer
C. the Floridian Aquifer

28. Who discovered that the universe is expanding?

A. Aristotle
B. Einstein
C. Hubble

29. Intrusive igneous rocks have

A. glassy textures
B. small crystals
C. large crystals

30. _____ measure vibrations in Earth.

A. scanning electron microscopes
B. tiltmeters
C. seismographs

31. The most common type of sand dune is the

A. barchan dune
B. parabolic dune
C. star dune

32. The mid-ocean ridge system is a major area of which type plate movement?

A. subduction
B. divergence
C. convergence

33. When lava cools quickly on Earth's surface the newly formed rock is called

A. clastic
B. intrusive
C. extrusive

34. Barrier islands form

A. perpendicular to the mainland
B. parallel to the mainland
C. thousands of miles away from the mainland

35. The process of research being scrutinized by independent qualified experts is known as

A. collaboration
B. peer review
C. scientific debate

36. Trenches observed on the sea floor are the result of

A. volcanoes
B. divergence
C. subduction

37. The limestone platform that builds up most of Florida's bedrock was formed during the

A. Cenozoic
B. Pre-Cambrian
C. Silurian

38. These massive waves are caused by the displacement of ocean water, and are often the result of underwater earthquakes.

A. epicenters
B. neap tides
C. tsunamis

39. Surface currents in the ocean are classified by

A. density
B. temperature
C. speed

40. Most cosmologists believe that Earth is the indirect result of a

A. black hole
B. implosion
C. supernova

41. A stream erodes bedrock by grinding sand and rock fragments against each other. This process is defined as:

A. dissolving
B. transportation
C. abrasion

42. Rocks formed from magma are

A. igneous
B. metamorphic
C. sedimentary

43. Rocks formed by the intense heating and/or compression of pre-existing rocks are classified as

A. igneous
B. metamorphic
C. sedimentary

44. Rocks made of loose materials that have been cemented together are

A. igneous
B. metamorphic
C. sedimentary

45. Glaciers produce

A. U-shaped valleys
B. V-shaped valleys
C. S-shaped valleys

46. On a station plot, a solid circle indicates

A. clear skies
B. partly cloudy skies
C. overcast skies

47. Which is the result of radioactive decay?

A. parent element
B. daughter element
C. half-life

48. The most abundant gas found in the atmosphere is

A. oxygen
B. nitrogen
C. CO_2

49. Which of the following areas of Florida is/are most susceptible to a raise in sea level?

A. the Keys
B. the panhandle
C. central Florida

50. Flat, elevated areas with steep sides are called

A. plains
B. mountains
C. plateaus

51. Arable land is _____ as we become more urbanized.

A. shrinking
B. drying out
C. growing

52. A hole that remains in the ground after a block of glacial ice melts is called a

A. pothole
B. sinkhole
C. kettle

53. Which type of volcano is built up of layers of lava flows?

A. composite volcano
B. shield volcano
C. cinder cone

54. Designed to protect properties from erosion, _____ may in fact have the opposite effect.

A. seawalls
B. channels
C. dredges

55. Changes in Earth's orbital properties may help explain

A. climate changes
B. wind patterns
C. changes in ocean currents

56. The major surface current that flows along the east coast of the United States is known as the

A. Bermuda Current
B. Mexican Current
C. Gulf Stream

57. Which of the following is NOT supporting evidence for plate tectonics?

A. shape of the continents
B. location of the continents
C. paleomagnetism

58. The most abundant solid found in sea water is

A. chloride
B. calcium carbonate
C. magnesium chloride

59. Seismic surveys can provide information about

A. earthquake risk
B. subsurface structures
C. the weather

60. A contour line that has tick pointing into the center indicates a

A. depression
B. mountain
C. valley

61. Fossils that can be used to date strata are called

A. datum fossils
B. index fossils
C. true fossils

62. Sediments can be _____ by fast moving water and _____ by slow moving water.

A. deposited, eroded
B. eroded, deposited
C. cemented, deposited

63. The layer of the atmosphere that shields earth from harmful ultraviolet radiation is called

A. ionic layer
B. ozone layer
C. equatorial layer

64. Which cannot travel through liquid?

A. body waves
B. P waves
C. S waves

65. The Sun transfers its heat to other objects by

A. conduction
B. radiation
C. convection

66. Which of the following makes it easiest to analyze and interpret data?

A. a table
B. a spreadsheet
C. a graph

67. A _____ is often found on the leeward side of a mountain range.

A. rain shadow
B. wind belt
C. land breeze

68. Continental crust is _____ than oceanic crust.

A. thicker
B. thinner
C. denser

69. An air mass that forms over the Gulf of Mexico would be called

A. polar
B. maritime
C. continental

70. Florida has been home to various aspects of the U.S. space program since

A. the early 1900s
B. the 1950s
C. the 1990s

71. Research and technology

A. never affect the public
B. never affect the economy
C. have an effect on both the public and the economy

72. Zones of very strong, moving air confined to narrow columns along the boundary between cold and warm air are called

A. jet streams
B. westerlies
C. prevailing winds

73. _____ is/are a climate phenomenon that affects weather patterns across the globe.

A. A monsoon
B. El Niño
C. The westerlies

74. The dark areas observed on the sun are known as

A. solar flares
B. prominences
C. sunspots

75. When one perceives and records an activity, this is called

A. assumption
B. inference
C. observation

76. A scale use to measure the hardness of a mineral is known as the

A. Bowen's scale
B. Mohs scale
C. Harding scale

77. When a liquid changes to a gas this process is known as

A. evaporation
B. condensation
C. dissolution

78. A fan-shaped river deposit is better known as a

A. levee
B. flood plain
C. delta

79. Florida experiences hurricanes mainly during the

A. spring and summer
B. winter and spring
C. summer and fall

80. Which of the following is used to separate light out into individual wavelengths?

A. spectrometer
B. radio telescope
C. interferometer

81. An explanation of events that occur with uniformity under the same conditions is a

A. law
B. theory
C. hypothesis

82. A(n) _____ shows no overall movement.

A. occluded front
B. stationary front
C. warm front

83. Surface ocean currents are caused by which of the following

A. temperature
B. density changes in water
C. wind

84. Higher elevations tend to be at _____ temperature than the surrounding area

A. a lower
B. a higher
C. the same

85. Much of Earth's _____ comes from outgassing at mid-ocean ridges.

A. oxygen
B. nitrogen
C. carbon

86. Chains of undersea mountains associated with seafloor spreading are known as _____.

A. ocean trenches
B. mid-ocean ridges
C. seamounts

87. When air blows from the cooler land onto the warmer sea at night it is called a

A. sea breeze
B. land breeze
C. monsoon

88. Closed contour lines on a topographic map indicate which of the following?

A. rivers and lakes
B. hills
C. mountains

89. Which of these scientists was famous for his laws of planetary motion?

A. Kepler
B. Copernicus
C. Aristotle

90. The phases of the Moon are the result of its _____ in relation to the Sun.

A. revolution
B. rotation
C. position

91. Which best describes the relationship between science and society?

A. science influences society
B. society influences science
C. society and science influence one another

92. The unit used to measure the distance between stars is called

A. astronomical unit
B. light-year
C. parsec

93. The largest planet found in the solar system is

A. Pluto
B. Jupiter
C. Saturn

94. If a fault cuts through an undeformed sedimentary bed, you can determine that

A. the fault is younger than the bed
B. the bed is younger than the fault
C. the bed and the fault are the same age

95. A resource that is replenished on a human timescale is called

A. infinite
B. non-renewable
C. renewable

96. A star's brightness is referred to as

A. magnitude
B. mass
C. apparent magnitude

97. Clouds of gas and dust where new stars originate are called

A. black holes
B. super novas
C. nebulae

98. The transfer of heat from Earth's surface to the atmosphere is called ____.

A. conduction
B. radiation
C. convection

99. Which of these measures small changes in the orientation of the ground surface?

A. tiltmeters
B. mass spectrometers
C. scanning electron microscopes

100. P waves

A. are surface waves
B. have a side to side motion
C. have a compressional motion

101. The Landsat program aims to collect information about

A. Earth viewed from space
B. volcanic activity
C. climate change

102. The level to which groundwater rises is known as

A. the water table
B. an aquifer
C. permeability

103. Which of the following is a method for investigating Earth's interior?

A. seismic tomography
B. tiltmeters
C. satellites

104. Who developed the Law of Gravitation?

A. Newton
B. Einstein
C. Kepler

105. The coal we use today began to form during the

A. Ordovician
B. Devonian
C. Carboniferous

106. The ratio of land to water affects

A. albedo
B. volcanism
C. plate tectonic motion

107. Rock pieces breaking off the edge of a cliff is an example of

A. mechanical weathering
B. chemical weathering
C. a lahar

108. Breaks in rocks along which materials suddenly move are called

A. fractures
B. folds
C. faults

109. The point underground at which rock breaks during an earthquake is called the

A. fault
B. epicenter
C. focus

110. The factor that will be measured in an experiment is the

A. constant
B. control
C. dependent variable

111. During which of the following time periods did a mass extinction occur?

A. Archaean
B. Triassic
C. Cretaceous

112. Energy derived from underground heat sources is known as

A. hydropower
B. geothermal
C. biomass energy

113. Most earthquakes originate in the

A. core
B. asthenosphere
C. lithosphere

114. Oxbow lakes may form from the action of

A. braided streams
B. meandering streams
C. chemical weathering

115. Runoff refers to

A. water running over the surface
B. water in the oceans
C. water evaporating from the ocean

116. Composite volcanoes are commonly found

A. at sea
B. along the "Ring of Fire"
C. nowhere near other volcanoes

117. Currently, most of our energy is supplied by _____.

A. nuclear power
B. fossil fuels
C. hydropower

118. Which type of telescope uses mirrors?

A. radio
B. refractor
C. reflector

119. Which of these rocks is likely to be found in continental crust?

A. basalt
B. granite
C. gabbro

120. What was the name of the 1998 mission to collect material from the comet Wild 2?

A. Cassini-Huygens
B. Stardust
C. Voyager

121. When scientists work together on a new idea, this is called

A. peer review
B. scientific debate
C. collaboration

122. Development and agriculture led to the loss of _____ of the Everglades wetland area.

A. 25%
B. 50%
C. 75%

123. The number 0.00005 contains _____ significant digit(s).

A. one
B. two
C. four

124. Who put forth the theory of continental drift, which led to the development of plate tectonic theory?

A. Wegener
B. Hubble
C. Milankovitch

125. The theory to explain the origin of the universe is known as?

A. Milankovitch Theory
B. Big Bang Theory
C. Newtonian Theory

Answer Key

1. A	45. A	89. A
2. C	46. C	90. C
3. C	47. B	91. C
4. B	48. B	92. C
5. B	49. A	93. B
6. C	50. C	94. A
7. C	51. A	95. C
8. C	52. C	96. A
9. B	53. B	97. C
10. C	54. A	98. A
11. B	55. A	99. A
12. A	56. C	100. C
13. A	57. B	101. A
14. C	58. A	102. A
15. A	59. B	103. A
16. A	60. A	104. A
17. B	61. B	105. C
18. C	62. B	106. A
19. B	63. B	107. A
20. B	64. C	108. C
21. A	65. B	109. C
22. B	66. C	110. C
23. A	67. A	111. C
24. B	68. A	112. B
25. A	69. B	113. C
26. C	70. B	114. B
27. C	71. C	115. A
28. C	72. A	116. B
29. C	73. B	117. B
30. C	74. C	118. C
31. A	75. C	119. B
32. B	76. B	120. B
33. C	77. A	121. C
34. B	78. C	122. B
35. B	79. C	123. A
36. C	80. A	124. A
37. A	81. A	125. B
38. C	82. B	
39. B	83. C	
40. C	84. A	
41. C	85. C	
42. A	86. B	
43. B	87. B	
44. C	88. B	

Rationales for Sample Questions

1. In which layer of the atmosphere would you expect most weather to occur?
A. troposphere
The troposphere is the lowest portion of Earth's atmosphere. It contains the highest amount of water and aerosol. Because it touches Earth's surface features, friction builds. For all of these reasons, weather is most likely to occur in the troposphere.

2. Which is the final stage in scientific inquiry?
C. communication
After the conclusion is drawn, the final step is communication. The conclusions must be communicated by clearly describing the information using accurate data, visual presentation (such as bar, line, or pie graphs), tables/charts, diagrams, artwork, and other appropriate media, such as a Power Point presentation.

3. Which layer of Earth's atmosphere contains the ozone layer?
C. stratosphere
The stratosphere is located above the troposphere and below the mesosphere. It has layers striated by temperature. The warmest portion, the ozone layer, absorbs solar ultraviolet radiation.

4. Which is the name for the model of the solar system developed by Copernicus?
B. heliocentric
Copernicus' model stated that the planets revolved around the Sun (heliocentric), as opposed to prior belief that the planets revolved around Earth (geocentric).

5. Qualitative research ends with
B. hypotheses and theories
Qualitative research ends with hypotheses and theories. The researcher is the instrument and the reasoning is inductive. There is minor use of numerical indices and the write up is descriptive.

6. The National Science Teacher's Association recommends limiting science classes to _____ or fewer students.
C. 24
The National Science Teachers Association recommendation is that science classes should be limited to 24 or fewer students.

7. A star's light and heat are produced by
C. nuclear fusion
Nuclear fusion is the process in which hydrogen atoms fuse together to form helium atoms, releasing massive amounts of energy. It's the fusion of atoms, not combustion, which causes stars to shine.

8. The goal of the TOPEX/Poseidon mission was to
C. map ocean surface topography
The goal of the TOPEX/Poseidon mission was to map ocean surface topography using satellites. The mission, which ran from 1992 until 2006 and was a joint NASA/Centre National d'Etudes Spatiales (CNES) venture, resulted in extensive data on sea level, global ocean topography, seasonal changes of ocean currents, phenomena such as El Niño and La Niña, the tides, and much more.

9. Rapid diversification of fish occurred in the
B. Devonian
The Devonian, also known as the "Age of Fishes," saw rapid diversification of fish species.

10. Which type of reef is a coral island with a central lagoon?
C. atoll
Atolls originally form as fringing reefs around small islands. If the central island is eroded, or subsides, the coral reef is left behind. Atolls are very common in the Pacific Ocean. Examples include Diego Garcia in the Indian Ocean and Midway Island in the Pacific Ocean.

11. Which is an example of a model?
B. the rock cycle
A model is a simplification or representation of a problem that is being studied or predicted. A model is a substitute, but it is similar to what it represents. The rock cycle is a model that describes the various complex geologic processes that create, destroy, and modify rocks.

12. Air flows from areas of _____ pressure to areas of _____ pressure.
A. high, low
Air flows from areas of high pressure to low pressure.

13. When molecules in the air cool and combine to form rain, _____ has occurred.
A. condensation
Condensation is the change in matter from a gas (or vapor) to a liquid. Rain is an example of condensation.

14. On a weather map, lines indicating constant pressure are called
C. isobars
Meteorologists use station plots to draw lines of constant pressure (isobars), temperature (isotherms), and dewpoint (isodrosotherms) to achieve an understanding of the current state of the atmosphere.

15. Florida's karst terrain is a result of
A. carbonate bedrock

Florida is underlain by carbonate rocks, which are susceptible to dissolution by water. This dissolution results in sinkholes, caves, springs, and underground streams, all of which are features of karst topography.

16. A yardang is formed by the erosive power of
A. wind

A yardang is a large, wind-sculpted landform with an orientation parallel to the direction of the prevailing wind.

17. On a topographic map, the points of a V representing a stream point
B. upstream

Stream valleys are represented by contour lines forming a V shape. The point of the V points in the upstream direction.

18. When the Sun, the Moon and Earth are aligned, what type of tide is produced?
C. spring tide

Spring tides are produced when Earth, the Sun, and the Moon are in a line. Therefore, spring tides occur during the full moon and the new moon. Neap tides occur during quarter moons. They occur when the gravitational forces of the Moon and the Sun are perpendicular to one another (with respect to Earth).

19. North of the equator, currents move in which direction?
B. clockwise

North of the equator, currents move clockwise. South of the equator, currents move counter-clockwise.

20. Rocks that serve as aquifers are
B. permeable

Aquifers are underground areas of permeable rock from which groundwater can be collected.

21. A narrow piece of land that juts out into the water is known as a
A. cape

A cape is a narrow piece of land that juts out into the water. Examples: Cape Cod, the Cape of Good Hope.

22. The expansion of desert-like conditions into adjacent areas is
B. desertification

Desertification occurs when poor land use practices result in the expansion of desert-like conditions into other areas. Desertification is a significant problem in the world's arid regions, where farmland may be destroyed as desert conditions take over.

23. Earth's outer core is probably
A. liquid
Earth's inner core is hypothesized to be solid iron and nickel. The outer core, surrounding the inner core, is believed to be molten iron.

24. If a geologist uses the principle of superposition to date a sequence of rocks, this is an example of
B. relative dating
The law of superposition states that in a sequence of undeformed sedimentary rocks, the oldest is at the bottom and the youngest is at the top. This law is only applicable to sedimentary rocks. This is an example of relative dating.

25. The San Andreas fault is classified as a
A. transform fault
The San Andreas fault is considered a transform fault because sections of Earth's crust (the Pacific and North American Plates) slide side-by-side past each other along the fault.

26. The New Horizons mission is currently on its way to
C. Pluto
The New Horizons mission launched in 2006 and is currently on its way to Pluto. It is estimated to near Pluto in 2015, at which point it will continue on into the Kuiper Belt to search for other Kuiper Belt objects.

27. Most of Florida's groundwater comes from
C. the Floridian Aquifer
Most of Florida's groundwater comes from the Floridian Aquifer, which provides the municipal water supply for several cities. It is one of the most productive aquifers in the world. The Biscayne Aquifer, located in the southeastern part of the state, is another important aquifer. Additionally, there are three other principal aquifers that provide drinking water for various areas of the state.

28. Who discovered that the universe is expanding?
C. Hubble
Edwin Hubble (1889-1953) was an American astronomer who drastically changed our view of space. Hubble discovered that he Milky Way is just one of millions of galaxies and that the universe itself is expanding. His ideas provided the first evidence for the Big Bang Theory, and he is often credited with being the father of cosmology.

29. Intrusive rocks have
C. large crystals
Intrusive igneous rocks have large crystals. This rock is formed from magma that cools and solidifies within Earth. Because it is surrounded by pre-existing rock, the magma cools slowly, and the rocks are coarse grained. The crystals are usually large enough to be seen by the unaided eye.

30. _____ measure vibrations in Earth.
C. seismographs
Seismographs record vibrations in Earth and allow scientists to measure earthquake activity.

31. The most common type of sand dune is the
A. barchan dune.
Crescent-shaped sand dunes with crescent horns pointing downwind are called barchan dunes. These develop in areas with limited sand supply and are usually separated from one another as they move across the bare ground. The barchan dune is the most common type of sand dune.

32. The mid-ocean ridge system is a major area of which type plate movement?
B. divergence
The mid-ocean ridge system is a result of seafloor spreading along divergent plate boundaries.

33. When lava cools quickly on Earth's surface the newly formed rock is called
C. extrusive
Rock formed by the cooling of magma on Earth's surface is known as extrusive, as opposed to intrusive, which is formed by the cooling of magma below Earth's surface.

34. Barrier islands form
B. parallel to the mainland
Barrier islands are located parallel to the mainland, separated by estuaries, bays, and/or lagoons, on a gently sloping continental shelf. These islands provide protection to the mainland from the brunt of ocean waves.

35. The process of research being scrutinized by independent qualified experts is known as
B. peer review
The peer review process means that before a scientific paper is published, it is scrutinized by independent qualified experts to ensure the validity and soundness of the ideas in the paper. This peer review process ensures that only high-quality research is published.

36. Trenches observed on the sea floor are the result of
C. subduction
Trenches are created where areas of oceanic and continental crust collide. Plate collision causes denser oceanic crust to sink or slip beneath lighter continental crust. This subduction produces a deep trench on the ocean floor parallel to the plate boundary.

37. The limestone platform that builds up most of Florida's bedrock was formed during the
A. Cenozoic

During the early Cenozoic, the Florida platform was submerged beneath the Tethys Sea. While the platform was submerged, the skeletons of billions of marine invertebrates were deposited, building up the limestone platform that forms much of Florida's bedrock.

38. These massive waves are caused by the displacement of ocean water, and are often the result of underwater earthquakes.
C. tsunamis

Earthquakes can trigger an underwater landslide or cause sea floor displacements that in turn, generate deep waves in all directions. Far out to sea these waves may be hardly noticeable. However, as they near the shoreline, the shallowing of the sea floor forces the waves upward in a "springing" motion.

39. Surface currents in the ocean are classified by
B. temperature

Surface currents are caused by winds and are classified by temperature.

40. Most cosmologists believe that Earth is the indirect result of a
C. supernova

Most cosmologists believe that Earth is the indirect result of a supernova. The thin cloud (planetary nebula) of gas and dust from which the Sun and its planets are formed, was struck by the shock wave and remnant matter from an exploded star(s) outside of our galaxy.

41. A stream erodes bedrock by grinding sand and rock fragments against each other. This process is defined as
C. abrasion

Abrasion is the key form of mechanical weathering. It is a sandblasting effect caused by particles of sand or sediment. Abrasive agents include wind blown sand, water movement, and the movement of materials in landslides.

42. Rocks formed from magma are
A. igneous

Igneous rocks are rocks that have formed from cooled magma. They are further classified as extrusive or intrusive according to where they cooled.

43. Rocks formed by the intense heating and/or compression of pre-existing rocks are classified as
B. metamorphic
Metamorphism is the process of changing a pre-existing rock into a new rock by heat and/or pressure. Metamorphism is similar to putting a clay pot into a kiln. The clay doesn't melt, but a solid-state chemical reaction occurs that causes a change. The chemical bonds of adjoining atoms breakdown and allow the atoms to rearrange themselves, producing a substance with new properties.

44. Rocks made of loose materials that have been cemented together are
C. sedimentary
Sediments are broken up rock material. Sand on a beach and pebbles in a mountain stream are typical examples. Sedimentary rocks are named for their source; they are rocks that form from sediments that lithify to become solid rock. Sedimentary rock is especially important for the finding of fossils.

45. Glaciers produce
A. U-shaped valleys
River valleys are typically V- shaped. The velocity and cutting power of a river is greatest at its center. However, glaciers broaden the area. Upon its retreat, a glacier typically leaves a U- shaped valley.

46. On a station plot, a solid circle indicates
C. overcast skies
A solid circle indicates overcast skies.

47. Which is the result of radioactive decay?
B. daughter element
Radioactive decay causes a parent isotope to decay into a daughter isotope. The half-life is the time it takes for half of the original, or parent isotope, to decay into its daughter product.

48. The most abundant gas found in the atmosphere is
B. nitrogen
The atmosphere is composed of 78% nitrogen, 21% oxygen, and 1% other gasses.

49. Which of the following areas of Florida is/are most susceptible to a raise in sea level?
A. the Keys
As sea level rises, Florida's coastal and low-lying areas may become inundated. A sea level rise of only a few meters would likely inundate the Florida Keys, cause significant flooding in the Everglades, and cover low lying coastal areas along both of Florida's coasts.

50. Flat, elevated areas with steep sides are called
C. plateaus
Plateaus are flat, elevated areas with steep sides, which encompass very large areas of Earth's surface.

51. Arable land is _____ as we become more urbanized.
A. shrinking
Arable farmland is shrinking as the pressure to develop home and commercial sites increases. Of the approximately 15 billion hectares of dry land on Earth, only 2 billion are suitable for agriculture. If the same land is used year after year, there is a definite danger of soil exhaustion as vital nutrients are depleted.

52. A hole that remains in the ground after a block of glacial ice melts is called a
C. kettle
Kettles are basins or depressions formed by isolate blocks of ice that later melt. When these depressions are filled with water they care called kettle lakes.

53. Which type of volcano is built up of layers of lava flows?
B. shield volcano
Shield volcanoes are built up of successive layers of basaltic lava flows.

54. Designed to protect properties from erosion, _____ may in fact have the opposite effect.
A. seawalls
Seawalls and riprap placed along shorelines are intended to protect property from erosion, but reflect wave energy back. This increased wave energy increases erosion of beaches in front of the seawall and may eventually cause undermining of the structure. Properties with riprap in front of them may one day lose their beach entirely.

55. Changes in Earth's orbital properties may help explain
A. climate changes
Changes in the shape of Earth's orbit (eccentricity), along with tilt and precession, affect the amount of sunlight the planet receives. These processes change according to cycles—100,000 years for eccentricity, 41,000 years for tilt, and 19,000-23,000 years for precession. According to a theory developed by Mulitin Milankovitch, a Serbian mathematician, these cycles can explain the occurrence of periodic ice ages.

56. The major surface current that flows along the east coast of the United States is known as the
C. Gulf Stream
The Gulf Stream begins in the Caribbean and ends in the northern North Atlantic. It is powerful enough to be seen from outer space and is one of the world's most studied current systems. It acts as the east coast boundary current plays an important role in the transfer of heat and salt to the poles.

57. Which of the following is NOT supporting evidence for plate tectonics?
B. location of the continents
Evidence supporting plate tectonic theory includes the shape of the continents, paleomagnetism, the age of rocks of the ocean floor, climatology, identical rock units across ocean basins, topographic evidence, fossil evidence, and sea turtle migrations.

58. The most abundant solid found in sea water is
A. chloride
Chloride is the most abundant solid in sea water. Sodium is the second most abundant.

59. Seismic surveys can provide information about
B. subsurface structures
Seismic surveys use seismic waves to obtain data about subsurface features and structures

60. A contour line that has tick pointing into the center indicates a
A. depression
Contour lines are shown as closed circles in elevated areas and as lines with miniature perpendicular lined edges where depressions exist.

61. Fossils that are used to date strata are called
B. index fossils
Index fossils are fossils of organisms that were known to be abundant at specific times in Earth's history. Presence of such fossils gives one an idea of what age the surrounding material came from.

62. Sediments can be _____ by fast moving water and _____ by slow moving water.
B. eroded, deposited
Fast moving water tends to erode sediments that may get deposited when the velocity decreases.

63. The layer of the atmosphere that shields earth from harmful ultraviolet radiation is called
B. ozone layer
The ozone layer is the part of Earth's atmosphere that contains high concentrations of ozone (O_3). It is located in the stratosphere and absorbs UV radiation emitted from the sun, making life possible on Earth.

64. Which cannot travel through liquid?
C. S waves
S waves are slower than P waves, and cannot travel through liquids. Therefore, they cannot travel through Earth's liquid outer core.

65. The Sun transfers its heat to other objects by
B. radiation
Radiation is the process by which energy is transferred in the form of waves or particles. The Sun emits ultraviolet radiation in UVA, UVB, and UVC forms, but because of the ozone layer, most of the ultraviolet radiation that reaches Earth's surface is UVA.

66. Which of the following makes it easiest to analyze and interpret data?
C. a graph
Graphs help scientists visualize and interpret variations and patterns in data, and are generally easier to interpret than tables or spreadsheets.

67. A _____ is often found on the leeward side of a mountain range.
A. rain shadow
Relief has a unique affect on climate as well. In mountainous areas a rain shadow effect may be noticed. The rain shadow effect refers to the fact that the windward sides of mountains tend to be very rainy, while the leeward sides are often quite dry.

68. Continental crust is _____ than oceanic crust.
A. thicker
Oceanic crust and continental crust have different physical and chemical compositions. Oceanic crust is denser and thinner than continental crust. It is mainly composed of mafic rocks like basalt and gabbro. Continental crust is thicker and less dense, and is composed mainly of felsic rocks like granite.

69. An air mass that forms over the Gulf of Mexico would be called
B. maritime
Maritime air masses are moist, containing considerable amounts of water vapor, which is ultimately condensed and released as rain or snow. Maritime air masses form over the ocean.

70. Florida has been home to various aspects of the U.S. space program since

B. the 1950s

The eastern coast of central Florida has been home to various aspects of the U.S. space program since the 1950s when it was first used as a missile launch site by the Air Force. Florida's role in the space program was solidified when NASA built the massive Kennedy Space Center, which has had a lasting effect on the region.

71. Research and technology

C. have an effect on both the public and the economy

The relationship among basic and applied research, technology, the economy, and society is such that each is interdependent on the others.

72. Zones of very strong, moving air confined to narrow columns along the boundary between cold and warm air are called

A. jet streams

Jet streams are zones of very strong, moving air confined to narrow columns and they mark the zones where the cold polar air and the warmer air meet. This produces the greatest pressure gradients. Jet streams can be either straight or dramatically dip, creating ridges and troughs on the 500-300mb pressure surface.

73. _____ is/are a climate phenomenon that affects weather patterns across the globe.

B. El Niño

El Niño is a reverse of the normal weather patterns in the Pacific. A low-pressure area normally sits in the Pacific Ocean west of Hawaii and a high-pressure area normally sits off of the California coast. When an El Niño forms, these pressure areas shift eastward, causing the low-pressure area to be situated below Hawaii and the high-pressure area to move inland over California. Because of the shift in pressure areas, an El Niño affects the wind patterns (especially the jet stream and trade winds), and creates a wide variety of effects, including a direct impact on commercial fishing.

74. The dark areas observed on the sun are known as

C. sunspots

Larger dark spots called sunspots appear regularly on the Sun's surface. These spots vary in size from small to 150,000 kilometers in diameter and may last from hours to months. The sunspots also cause solar flares that can accelerate to velocities of 900 km/hr, sending shock waves through the solar atmosphere.

75. When one perceives and records an activity, this is called

C. observation

Observation occurs when one perceives activity and records that activity.

76. A scale use to measure the hardness of a mineral is known as the
B. Mohs scale
The Mohs scale of hardness measures the scratch resistance of minerals relative to one another and other substances. The hardest material is diamond, and the softest is talc.

77. When a gas changes to a liquid this process is known as
A. evaporation
Evaporation is the change in matter from a liquid to a gaseous state. For example, water evaporates off the ocean surface into the atmosphere.

78. A fan-shaped river deposit is better known as a
C. delta
Flowing water carries suspended material to a quieter body of water, such as the ocean, where it deposits its load, forming a delta.

79. Florida experiences hurricanes mainly during the
C. summer and fall
During the summer and fall (June-November), Florida may experience tropical storms and hurricanes that form in the Atlantic Ocean.

80. Which of the following is used to separate light out into individual wavelengths?
A. spectrometer
Spectroscopy involves the study of light emitted by an object. Spectrometers are used to separate light out into its individual wavelengths, which creates a light spectrum. An object's spectrum can reveal much about its composition, temperature, density, and motion, so spectroscopy is a very useful tool in astronomy.

81. An explanation of events that occur with uniformity under the same conditions is a
A. law
A law is an explanation of events that occur with uniformity under the same conditions (laws of nature, law of gravity).

82. A(n) _____ shows no overall movement.
B. stationary front
Fronts are the boundaries where one air mass meets another. A stationary front is a boundary between two air masses, neither of which is strong enough to displace the other.

83. Surface ocean currents are caused by which of the following
C. wind

A current is a large mass of continuously moving oceanic water. Surface ocean currents are mainly wind-driven and occur in all of the world's oceans (example: the Gulf Stream). This is in contrast to deep ocean currents which are driven by changes in density.

84. Higher elevations tend to be at _____ temperature than the surrounding area
A. a lower

Higher elevations are generally colder, and lower elevations are generally hotter. Higher elevations that experience freezing temperatures, or where air masses are forced to heights where the air temperature is freezing, will experience snow, sleet, or hail more often than lower elevations.

85. Much of Earth's _____ comes from outgassing at mid-ocean ridges.
C. carbon

Unlike surface currents, deep ocean currents are driven by changes in density. These density differences may be caused by changes in salinity (halocline) or temperature (thermocline). Colder water sinks below warmer waters, causing a river (current) flowing below the warmer waters.

86. Chains of undersea mountains associated with seafloor spreading are known as
B. mid-ocean ridges

Mid-ocean ranges are underwater mountains formed by plate tectonics. The underwater mountains are all connected, making a single mid-oceanic ridge system that is the longest mountain range in the world. The ridges are active spreading sites with new magma constantly emerging.

87. When air blows from the cooler land onto the warmer sea at night it is called a
B. land breeze

A land breeze occurs when the land surface cools off in the evening, causing airflow to move from the cool land to the warmer sea.

88. Closed contour lines on a topographic map indicate which of the following?
B. hills

The rules of contouring dictate that contour lines are closed around hills, basins, or depressions. Because we know that depressions are shown using hachure marks, a closed contour line without such marks represents a hill.

89. Which of these scientists was famous for his laws of planetary motion?
A. Kepler
Danish astronomer Johannes Kepler (1571-1630) postulated what are now known as Kepler's Laws of Planetary Motion. The significance of Kepler's Laws is that they overthrew the ancient concept of uniform circular motion, which was a major support for the geocentric theory.

90. The phases of the Moon are the result of its _____ in relation to the Sun.
C. position
The Moon is visible in varying amounts during its orbit around Earth. One half of the Moon's surface is always illuminated by the Sun (appears bright), but the amount observed from Earth can vary from a full moon to none (a new moon).

91. Which best describes the relationship between science and society?
C. society and science influence one another
Science and society are closely intertwined, and each has a role in influencing the other.

92. The unit used to measure the distance between stars is called
C. parsec
Parsecs are the units used to describe the distance between stars. Astronomical units (AU) are used to describe the distances between celestial objects (example Earth is 1.00 ± 0.02 AU from the Sun). Light years are a unit of length measuring the distance light travels in a vacuum in one year.

93. The largest planet found in the solar system is
B. Jupiter
The planets (in decreasing size) are Jupiter, Saturn (body—not inclusive of rings), Uranus, Neptune, Earth, Venus, Mars, and Mercury. (Pluto was thought to be the smallest planet, but is no longer classified as a planet).

94. If a fault cuts through an undeformed sedimentary bed, you can determine that
A. the fault is younger than the bed
Using the principle of cross-cutting relationships, you can determine that the fault must be younger than the bed it cuts.

95. A resource that is replenished on a human timescale is called
C. renewable
A renewable resource is a resource that is capable of replenishment or regeneration on a human timescale.

96. A star's brightness is referred to as
A. magnitude

Magnitude is a measure of a star's brightness. The brighter the object appears, the lower the number value of its magnitude. The apparent magnitude is how bright an observer perceives the object to be. Mass has to do with how much matter can be measured, not brightness.

97. Clouds of gas and dust where new stars originate are called
C. nebulae

Nebulae are where new stars are born. They are large areas of gasses and dust. When the conditions are right, particles combine to form stars.

98. The transfer of heat from Earth's surface to the atmosphere is called
A. conduction

Radiation is the process of warming through rays or waves of energy, such as the Sun warms earth. Earth returns heat to the atmosphere through conduction. This is the transfer of heat through matter, such that areas of greater heat move to areas of less heat in an attempt to balance temperature.

99. Which of these measures small changes in the orientation of the ground surface?
A. tiltmeters

Tiltmeters are used to measure small changes in the orientation or tilt of the ground surface or of a structure. In Earth science, tiltmeters are useful for monitoring changes in the ground surface in seismically or volcanically active areas.

100. P waves
C. have a compressional motion

P waves are body waves. They are also called compressional waves because they push and pull in the direction they are moving.

101. The Landsat program aims to collect information about
A. Earth viewed from space

The Landsat program, a joint mission of NASA and the USGS, is a series of satellite missions to collect information about Earth as viewed from space. The Landsat program has greatly aided the science of remote sensing. The program has been collecting and archiving photographs of Earth since the early 1970s, providing an opportunity for scientists to view and evaluate changes in Earth's surface over time.

102. The level to which groundwater rises is known as
A. the water table

A water-bearing rock body that is able to transmit water to wells and springs is known as an aquifer, and the level that the groundwater will rise to within the soil is known as the water table.

103. Which of the following is a method for investigating Earth's interior?
A. seismic tomography
Seismic tomography uses seismic waves to develop three-dimensional views of Earth

104. Who developed the Law of Gravitation?
A. Newton
A major contribution by Newton was his Law of Gravitation, which states that every object attracts every other object with a force that for any two objects is directly proportional to the mass of each object. In simpler terms, objects with mass attract one another.

105. The coal we use today began to form during the
C. Carboniferous
The Carboniferous period is named for the rich deposits of coal that occur in strata of this age.

106. The ratio of land to water affects
A. albedo
There are differences in albedo (the amount of energy reflected by a surface) between land and water. The ratio of land to water, especially in the lower latitudes, therefore has an effect on the amount of solar energy reflected or absorbed.

107. Rock pieces breaking off the edge of a cliff is an example of
A. mechanical weathering
Mechanical (or physical) weathering occurs when rock is broken into smaller pieces with no change in chemical or mineralogical composition. The resulting material still resembles the original material. Example: Rock pieces breaking off of a boulder. The pieces still resemble the original material, but on a smaller scale.

108. Breaks in rocks along which materials suddenly move are called
C. faults
Faults are fractures along which materials suddenly move. The San Andreas fault is an example of a famous fault.

109. The point underground at which rock breaks during an earthquake is called the
C. focus
The point deep underground where the rock breaks is called the focus. The point on the surface directly above the focus is called the epicenter.

110. The factor that will be measured in an experiment is the
C. dependent variable
The dependent variable is the factor that will be measured in an experiment. It is called dependent variable since its outcome is dependent on the independent variables.

111. During which of the following time periods did a mass extinction occur?
C. Cretaceous
At the end of the Cretaceous Period there was a massive extinction event that was responsible for wiping out the dinosaurs.

112. Energy derived from underground heat sources is known as
B. geothermal
Geothermal energy is derived from natural underground sources of steam and hot water. Geothermal energy can be used to provide hot water as well as to produce electricity.

113. Most earthquakes originate in the
C. lithosphere
Comprised of the crust and uppermost part of the mantle, the lithosphere consists of cool, rigid, and brittle materials. Most earthquakes originate in the lithosphere.

114. Oxbow lakes may form from the action of
B. meandering streams
Sometimes a meandering stream erodes its channel in a way that cuts off one of the meander bends, eventually leaving it abandoned. When a meander becomes completely cut off from the main flow of the river, it is called and oxbow lake.

115. Runoff refers to
A. water running over the surface
Runoff refers to the process of water traveling over the surface to a river, lake, ocean, etc. Runoff carries water from rainfall and snowmelt along the surface to a larger body of water, where it rejoins the cycle of evaporation and precipitation again.

116. Composite volcanoes are commonly found
B. along the "Ring of Fire"
Composite volcanoes are common along the "Ring of Fire," where active subduction is occurring. Their explosivity makes them extremely dangerous volcanoes.

117. Currently, most of our energy is supplied by _____.
B. fossil fuels
Fossil fuels—coal, oil, and natural gas—comprise more than 85% of the energy used in the United States. They are formed from the remains of animals and plants that lived hundreds of millions of years ago, and are considered a non-renewable resource because the supply is limited.

118. Which type of telescope uses mirrors?
C. reflector
Reflector telescopes are optical devices that make use of a mirror or mirrors, to reflect light waves to an eyepiece (ocular), thereby eliminating chromatic aberrations. There are different types of reflector telescopes; some use mirrors only, and others make use of both lenses and mirrors.

119. Which of these rocks is likely to be found in continental crust?
B. granite
Oceanic crust is denser and thinner than continental crust. It is mainly composed of mafic rocks like basalt and gabbro. Continental crust is thicker and less dense, and is composed mainly of felsic rocks like granite.

120. What was the name of the 1998 mission to collect material from the comet Wild 2?
B. Stardust
Launched in 1998, the mission of Stardust was to collect material from the comet Wild 2 and its coma. It returned in 2006. This mission marked the first time that collected physical specimens have been returned to Earth from a location other than the Moon.

121. When scientists work together on a new idea, this is called
C. collaboration
Often scientists will collaborate when working on new ideas. Input from several different scientists, especially if from different (but related) disciplines, can greatly enhance the development of new ideas.

122. Development and agriculture led to the loss of _____ of the Everglades wetland area.
B. 50%
The building of roads, canals, and levees to support agriculture and development have altered the natural water flow pattern of the Everglades, leading to the loss of 50% of its wetland areas and unique habitats, as well as other ecological functions.

123. The number 0.00005 contains _____ significant digit(s).
A. one
Zeros to the left of the first nonzero digit are not significant. Example: 0.0002 contains one significant digit.

124. Who put forth the theory of continental drift, which led to the development of plate tectonic theory?
A. Wegener

In 1906, Alfred Wegener became intrigued by how the shape of the continents indicated that they at one time fit together. Wegener became convinced that the landmasses had—at one point in history—been connected, forming a giant supercontinent that he later dubbed Pangea. Most of his data and evidence is still included in the proofs offered for modern tectonic theory. Not surprisingly, his controversial theory of moveable continents was not readily accepted. Modern geology owes much to Alfred Wegener's initial postulations. The advent of new technologies has made it possible for science to verify most of his observations, and additional, new data has expanded Wegener's original concept into the widely accepted, modern theory of tectonics.

125. The theory to explain the origin of the universe is known as?
B. Big Bang Theory

The Big Bang Theory proposes that all the mass and energy of the universe was originally concentrated at a single geometric point and, for unknown reasons, experienced a massive explosion that scattered the matter throughout the universe. The concept of a massive explosion is supported by the distribution of background radiation and the measurable fact that the galaxies are moving away from each other at great speed.

XAMonline, INC. 21 Orient Ave. Melrose, MA 02176

Toll Free number 800-509-4128

TO ORDER Fax 781-662-9268 OR www.XAMonline.com

FLORIDA TEACHER CERTIFICATION
EXAMINATIONS   - FTCE - 2008

PO#   Store/School:

Bill to Address 1   Ship to address

City, State Zip

Credit card number_____-_____-_____-_____   expiration_____

EMAIL _____

PHONE   FAX

13# ISBN 2007	TITLE	Qty	Retail	Total
978-1-58197-900-8	Art Sample Test K-12			
978-1-58197-689-2	Biology 6-12			
978-1-58197-046-3	Chemistry 6-12			
978-1-58197-047-0	Earth/Space Science 6-12			
978-1-58197-578-9	Educational Media Specialist PK-12			
978-1-58197-347-1	Elementary Education K-6			
978-1-58197-292-4	English 6-12			
978-1-58197-274-0	Exceptional Student Ed. K-12			
978-1-58197-294-8	FELE Florida Ed. Leadership			
978-1-58197-619-9	French Sample Test 6-12			
978-1-58197-615-1	General Knowledge			
978-1-58197-586-4	Guidance and Counseling PK-12			
978-1-58197-045-6	Humanities K-12			
978-1-58197-640-3	Mathematics 6-12			
978-1-58197-597-0	Middle Grades English 5-9			
978-1-58197-662-5	Middle Grades General Science 5-9			
978-1-58197-286-3	Middle Grades Integrated Curriculum			
978-1-58197-284-9	Middle Grades Math 5-9			
978-1-58197-590-1	Middle Grades Social Science 5-9			
978-1-58197-616-8	Physical Education K-12			
978-1-58197-044-9	Physics 6-12			
978-1-58197-657-1	Prekindergarten/Primary PK-3			
978-1-58197-695-3	Professional Educator			
978-1-58197-659-5	Reading K-12			
978-1-58197-270-2	Social Science 6-12			
978-1-58197-583-3	Spanish K-12			
			SUBTOTAL	
ndling $8.25 one title, $11.00 two titles, $15.00 three or more titles				
			TOTAL	

CPSIA information can be obtained at www.ICGtesting.com

230322LV00001B/51/P